Native and Naturalized
Trees
of New England
and Adjacent Canada

# Native and Naturalized

# Trees

## of New England
## and Adjacent Canada

A FIELD GUIDE

Richard M. DeGraaf and Paul E. Sendak

University Press of New England
Hanover and London

Published by University Press of New England,
One Court Street, Lebanon, NH 03766
www.upne.com
© 2006 by University Press of New England
Printed in the United States of America
5  4  3  2  1

Library of Congress Cataloging-in-Publication Data
DeGraaf, Richard M.
Native and naturalized trees of New England and adjacent Canada :
a field guide / Richard M. DeGraaf and Paul E. Sendak.
        p.    cm.
Includes bibliographical references and index.
ISBN-13: 978-1-58465-545-9 (paperback : alk. paper)
ISBN-10: 1-58465-545-3 (pbk. : alk. paper)
1. Trees—New England—Identification.
2. Trees—Canada, Eastern—Identification.
3. Trees—New England—Pictorial works.
4. Trees—Canada, Eastern—Pictorial works.
I. Sendak, Paul E.  II. Title.
QK121.D44 2006
582.160974—dc22                                        2005035960

*To Benjamin B. "Prof" Stout,*

*beloved teacher and advisor*

*at Rutgers University*

# Contents

# Acknowledgments

Ellen Wicklum suggested this book, Anna M. Lester prepared the tree illustrations and distribution maps, and Dennis W. Magee critically reviewed the manuscript. Symbols for leaf shape and arrangement were prepared by Nancy Haver, book design was by Michael Burton, and Mary A. Strong typed the manuscript. Susan Campbell of the Massachusetts Woodlands Institute facilitated publication. Our sincerest thanks to all.

# Introduction

New England and adjacent Canada encompass a wide range of environmental conditions due to the region's dramatic latitudinal and elevational gradients. Extending from the tree line in Canada and the high peaks of northern and central New England to sheltered southern coastal environs, the region contains the most northerly species of trees in North America and southern trees at the northern limits of their distribution. With its wide range of climatic conditions and soils, and long settlement history, New England and Maritime Canada contain many planted tree specimens from around the world.

We include here the native and naturalized trees—those introduced species that have been established as populations of the region. We intend this book as an easy-to-use field guide for all who encounter an unfamiliar tree in the forest and wonder what kind it is.

A tree is here defined as a large woody perennial plant, typically having a single upright trunk, and a well-defined crown. A shrub is a woody, perennial plant differing from a tree in its lower height and general absence of a well-defined main stem. There is no clear distinction between small trees and large shrubs; each varies in height depending upon age and local growing conditions.

Though arbitrary, the distinction is useful, and shrubs constitute a significant component of the overall forest vegetation, especially in moist woodlands, wooded wetlands, and highly disturbed sites. Species including bladdernut (*Staphlea trifolia*), scrub or bear oak (*Quercus illicifolia*), witch-hazel (*Hammamelis virginiana*), various hawthorns (*Crataegus* sp.), alternate-leaf dogwood (*Cornus alternifolia*), and nannyberry (*Viburnum lentago*), among others, are sometimes found growing as small trees up to 5 or 6 m tall. Most provide food for birds and mammals. Likewise, species such as willows (*Salix* sp.), sumacs (*Rhus* sp.), blueberries (*Vaccinium* sp.), viburnums (*Viburnum* sp.), silky dogwood (*C. amomum*), gray dogwood (*C. racemosa*), and brambles (*Rubus* sp.) often grow in thickets and provide food and cover for deer, grouse, woodcock, and many other small mammals and birds. These species, though important, are not included here.

**Tree Names.** In each account, the common English name in the northeastern United States, from D. Magee and H. Ahles's *Flora of the Northeast,* is given first; other common names follow. The scientific name, family name, and French name for trees occurring in Canada, after J. L. Farrar, *Trees of the Northern United States and Canada,* are also included. In several cases, Magee and Ahles use species names that differ from those in other accepted sources. We have included the other, often more familiar, names in brackets after the scientific name where this discrepancy exists.

### Tree Identification

A tree can be identified in several ways. The most popular method—and the least scientific—is to compare the tree with pictures in a guide. This is inefficient and confusing because most guides or manuals illustrate trees for a vast area—North America, for example—and many more are shown than occur in a given local area. Comparison with reference specimens in an herbarium is useful but only to those with access to an herbarium and who know how to use one. Going to the field with an expert or bringing a twig to one is reliable, but does not teach one how to go about identifying new trees on one's own. Formal courses in plant identification use keys to distinguishing characters to separate genera and species. Considerable time and effort are required to learn how keys are structured and to master the technical terminology they contain. This book uses a different approach for non-specialists. Trees are separated into conifer and broadleaf categories, which anyone will recognize, and then uses leaf shape and arrangement groups to narrow the possibilities when identifying a new tree.

The individual tree accounts contain descriptors of the species, some ecological relationships, notes on other aspects or uses of the tree, and a short list of characteristics for quick field identification. All trees are illustrated with line drawings. Distribution maps are provided only for native tree species. Naturalized species are too local or dispersed to map. The primary bases for classifying all seed-producing plants, including trees, are the reproductive features—the flowers and cones. The flowering stage of trees, however, is brief, and the characteristics of flowers are available for identification in the field only for a short time. Therefore, for our purposes other characteristics must be used—leaves, twigs, bark, buds, or fruit—to separate one species from another. We have for the most part used non-technical terms in the species accounts.

**Size and form** refer to the general appearance of the species. Individual specimens vary as well due to age, climate, and soil conditions. Young trees tend to have narrow crowns that spread with age; trees on fertile moist sites tend to grow faster than individuals of the same species on poor or dry sites. Also, injuries due to wind, insects, fire, or ice storms may alter crown shape considerably. These factors, in addition to the tree's individual genetic makeup, contribute to the observed variation in size and growth form within species. Also, a consistent form or growth habit may not be observed throughout the region. Despite these factors, growth form does become fairly useful as one becomes experienced in observing the stem and branch patterns that typify each species. Many tree species have such distinctive growth form that they can be identified at a glance, even at great distance. Examples are the vase-shaped American elm, the pin oak with its retained dead lower branches, or white pine, with its horizontal branches and its often greater height than that of adjacent hardwoods of the same age.

Growth form of the trunk and crown are influenced greatly by whether the tree grew in the open or in the forest. Open-grown trees normally have relatively thick, often crooked and sometimes forked trunks; low branches, and large, wide-spreading crowns. Forest-grown trees tend to have fairly slender, long, straight, commonly unforked trunks that are free of branches for a considerable height, and short, narrow crowns. The diameter of the trunk is measured at breast height, 1.3 meters or 4.5 feet above the ground.

**Leaves** are important in distinguishing among species because of their characteristic shapes and arrangement on the shoot. Like growth form, leaves are also variable, sometimes out of reach, and, for deciduous species, only available part of the year. Still, they can be used to separate all but the most similar or closely related species. Leaves are usually quite variable in size within a species due to such factors as tree age and health, the type and location of the shoot bearing the leaves, and the conditions under which the tree or twig is growing—sun or shade, among other factors. Leaves in the upper and center crown that are exposed to full sunlight are called *sun leaves,* and are normally smaller, thicker, and more shiny than *shade leaves* of the lower and interior crown. Some species such as oaks and maples show great differences between sun and shade leaves, so size alone is not a good diagnostic characteristic.

Leaves of deciduous trees are more variable than those of conifers, which, with the exception of larches, are present on the tree year-round.

The various leaf characteristics that are useful in tree identification include:

Leaf arrangement on the twig: alternate or opposite

Leaf type: simple or compound

Leaf size: leaf length and width for simple leaves; leaflet size and shape (pinnate or palmate) for compound leaves

Leaf blade shape at tip and base (fig. I.1)

Leaf margin: entire, serrate, lobed, etc. (fig. I.2)

Leaf texture and color of upper and lower surfaces

Venation, vein pattern

Petiole size, shape, stipules, etc.

Autumn color

Leaf size and shape are important descriptors for most species, but size is often very variable within a species, and for some species, such as the mulberries or sassafras, shape is variable on the same tree. When using leaves to identify a tree, it is useful to look at the most obvious characters first. Are the leaves in an alternate or opposite arrangement on the twig? Are they simple or compound? If leaves are out of reach, the branch pattern of the outer limb will normally reveal the leaf arrangement: buds arise in leaf axils, so species with opposite leaves will also have opposite branches.

**Bark** characteristics, especially on mature trees, can be a useful feature—sometimes some of the most important features in tree identification. Unlike leaves, flowers, or fruits, bark is available for comparison year-round. The importance of

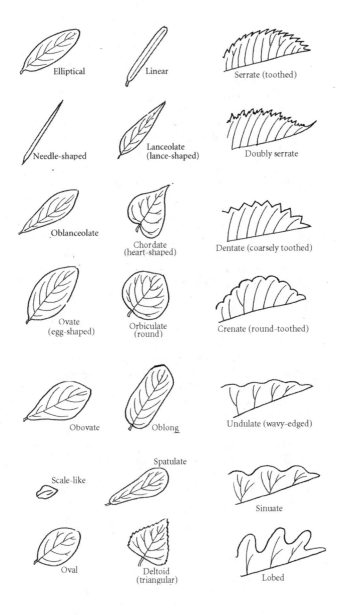

Figure I.1. Leaf shapes.

Figure I.2. Leaf margins.

bark is such that foresters, arborists, and others who work with trees often rely almost entirely on bark characteristics to aid in tree identification. Bark characteristics are best learned by direct observation. Though distinctive, bark is difficult to describe and illustrate. Furthermore, characteristics change dramatically with age and growth rate for most species. All trees have smooth bark when young; the color and size of pores—soft corky spots and lines called *lenticels*—are important distinguishing features of certain young trees with smooth bark, such as cherry and apple. A few species such as American beech, trembling aspen, and pin cherry retain smooth bark with age. Most trees soon develop roughened, scaly, furrowed, or platy bark which first appears at the bottom of the trunk and spreads upward with age.

When using bark for field identification, the primary features to examine are thickness, the type and degree of surface texture (whether smooth, scaly, furrowed, platy, or peeling); the color of the outer (and sometimes inner) bark, the relative length and width of plates, and the degree to which ridges intersect. Some examples of bark features used to distinguish among similar species are the long vertical plates of red oak compared to the short black plates of black oak. The fairly thin, closely fissured bark of Norway maple contrasts with the deeply furrowed, thick platy bark of sugar maple. Becoming familiar with the bark characteristics of related species is a great help in tree identification.

**Twigs,** the woody terminal ends of branches, no longer bear leaves but contain leaf scars and provide good identification characteristics throughout the year, except for a brief period in spring when buds formed the previous year are opening and new ones have not yet developed. The primary features used in identification are twig diameter, whether slender or stout; form: straight, zigzag, etc.; hairiness: whether there are prickles, spines, or thorns; leaf or stipule scars; bundle traces; pith characteristics, whether continuous, chambered, or diaphragmed; and other features of the surface such as a peeling, warty, or corky surface. When a leaf falls from a twig, a leaf scar remains where it was attached. Leaf scar size and shape are consistent within species. Where veins passed between leaf and twig, vein scars (bundle traces) remain as small dots, often in characteristic patterns within the leaf scar that are useful in identification. The central core of

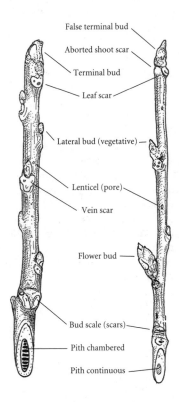

False terminal bud

Aborted shoot scar

Terminal bud

Leaf scar

Lateral bud (vegetative)

Lenticel (pore)

Vein scar

Flower bud

Bud scale (scars)

Pith chambered

Pith continuous

Figure I.3. Examples of winter twigs: (left) black walnut, (right) American elm. After B. V. Barnes and W. H. Wagner, Jr. 2002. *Trees of Michigan.* University of Michigan Press, Ann Arbor.

the twig is composed of *pith,* which usually differs in color and texture from the adjacent wood, and readily observed if the twig is cut. When the twig is cut across, it may appear star-shaped, as in oaks, or round, as in ash. A twig cut lengthwise reveals whether the pith is solid or *continuous, diaphragmed* with regularly spaced disks separating solid sections, or chambered with regularly spaced partitions separating hollow sections. Such patterns are species-specific and very useful in identification (fig. I.3).

**Buds** are the undeveloped shoots and leaves and their protective scales. In spring, the outer scales are shed, the preformed leaves enlarge, and the shoot begins to elongate. Some buds produce flowers. Buds are most important for identification in late autumn and winter, but can be useful for much of the year once they have formed. Their size, shape, arrangement, degree of hairiness, and the type and number of outer scales are important identifying features. All trees and shrubs have lateral buds on the sides of the shoot. These buds form the axils of the leaf petioles, and in fall and winter appear at the leaf scars. They may be pressed against the twig (*appressed*) or diverge from it in varying degrees (*divergent*). All species have a bud at the end of the new growth, but not all end buds are true terminal buds. In some species the end bud is actually a lateral bud because the end of the shoot dies back and is shed at the last mature lateral bud, leaving a false terminal bud at the twig end. Such is the case in birches, willows, and elms, for example. Lateral buds usually are similar to terminal buds, but smaller. Flower buds often differ in size and shape from terminal buds.

**Flowers** are normally the best features for plant identification and classification because they are much less variable than leaves, bark, or other characteristics within species. For the purposes of this guide, however, they are not so

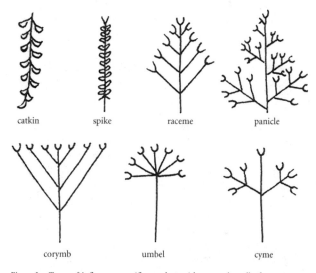

catkin    spike    raceme    panicle

corymb    umbel    cyme

Figure I.4. Types of inflorescences (flower clusters) borne on broadleaf trees.

useful because they generally are unavailable, being located in the upper crown, appearing rather briefly in spring, and generally being so small that they must be observed with magnification. We describe the flowers in general terms, emphasizing the type of flower cluster or *inflorescence* rather than the structure of individual flowers, because the structure of flower clusters is rather readily observed, such as the catkins of birches or oaks or the slender panicle of mountain maple (fig. I.4). Conifers do not produce a flower; for these species we describe the immature cones.

**Fruits and cones,** the seed-bearing parts of flowering plants and conifers, respectively, are very important in identifying trees and are described in some detail. Characteristics of the fruit or cone are normally among the key identifying features of each species. Fruits and cones usually are more available than flowers, stay on the tree longer, and, when found shed beneath a tree may be ascribed more readily to that tree than wind-blown leaves. Fruits and cones vary little among individuals within a species.

In conifers of our region, the seeds are borne in woody cones. Among flowering plants, the seeds are borne in fruits of various kinds, depending on how the ovary walls containing the seed develop: with a thin papery wing or *samara,* as in elms or ashes; a strong inner wall and fleshy outer part, as in the *drupe* of cherries or black gum; or mostly fleshy *berry* or *pome* as in blueberry and apple. Some dry fruits split along suture lines and include the *capsules* of black willow; those that do not split are *nuts* or *samaras.* Becoming familiar with the various fruit types and the differences among similar types such as oak *acorns* are a great help in separating tree species that otherwise may look similar (fig. I.5).

We provide brief descriptions of tree species natural **distributions**. These descriptions are of species' total ranges, usually with details for our region. We also provide general descriptions of the **habitat** in which a given tree generally or typically is found. Some species such as red maple are widespread and occur naturally in both wet or dry sites. Others such as black gum are quite narrow in the types of natural habitats in which they occur. For some trees, associated trees, shrubs, and herbaceous plants are definitive. Its distribution and the habitat in which a naturally occurring tree is found are useful initial guides to an unfamiliar tree's identity.

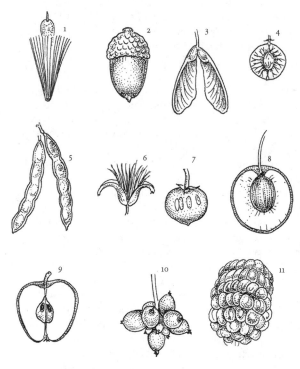

Figure I.5. Fruit types of broadleaf trees: (1) an *achene* from the globose multiple of *achenes* (sycamore); (2) *acorn* (oak); (3) paired *samaras* (maple); (4) single *samara* (elm); (5) *pod* or *legume* (black locust); (6) *capsule* (willow); (7) *berry* halved (grape); (8) *drupe* (black cherry); (9) *pome* halved (apple); (10) cluster of *drupes* (dogwood); (11) aggregate of *drupes* (red mulberry). After B. V. Barnes and W. H. Wagner, Jr. 2002. *Trees of Michigan.* University of Michigan Press, Ann Arbor.

We include **notes** on a wide range of information about species that, while not pertinent to identification, provides details on its ecology, wood properties and past or present uses of the wood, the origins of its scientific name, or aspects of its life history.

The "In the Field" section of each entry gives key characters that enable ready identification. Comparison with similar species is noted for characteristics that are especially useful in separating them.

### *Organization for Leaf-on (Summer) Identification*

This book is organized by tree types that combine several identifying features, for example, whether coniferous or broadleaf, and leaf type and arrangement on the stem or twig. These categories are identified by symbols that are shown below and that appear as thumb tabs that separate sections of the book. Once familiar with these symbols, you can systematically find the one for the section containing your tree, and look through the accounts therein to identify it.

First locate the appropriate section and find the correct symbol by characterizing your tree: conifer or broadleaf? If a conifer, are the needles in a cluster, single, or scaly? If broadleaf, is the leaf shape simple, lobed, or compound, and are the leaves arranged on the twig opposite one another or in alternate pattern? Browse through the illustrations in the tree accounts in that section to find your tree. Examine the illustration and read the accompanying text to confirm your identification.

### *Step-by-step Identification Details*

Trees in this guide are grouped initially into two main types: coniferous and broadleaf trees.

Trees with (usually) evergreen, needle-like leaves that remain on the tree all year and have seed-bearing cones are conifers. The one exception is tamarack, a conifer that annually sheds its needles in autumn. Trees with wide flat leaves that are shed each autumn are broadleaf. Again, there is one exception, American holly, which retains its broad, evergreen leaves all year. Also, oak, especially young oak trees, usually retain many of their dry brown leaves well into winter. Conifers are shown in the first part of the book, followed by broadleaf trees.

The text also gives details of bark, buds, fruits or nuts, and twig characteristics that will enable you to identify the tree in winter, when deciduous trees are bare. In any season, the map will be of use to indicate whether the tree is likely found in your area.

### *Leaf Type*

**Conifers: Bunched, Bundled, or Scaly (Flattened) Needles**
For conifers, distinguish among needles in bunches on spur shoots, or single, bundled, or scaly (flattened) needles. Note the

number of needles that arise from one point on the twig. If only one needle, these trees are shown in group 2. If in bundles of at least two, consult the bundled needles section, noting how many needles per bundle; the section progresses from two needles (group 3) to five per cluster (group 5). Trees with scaly (flattened), overlapping needles are shown in group 6.

## Broadleaf Trees: Simple, Not Lobed, Lobed, or Compound Leaves

For broadleaf trees, distinguish among the several leaf shapes or types. The broadleaf tree groups are arranged in order of leaf shape: those with simple leaves without lobes are first, followed by those with lobed, pinnately compound, doubly compound, and palmately compound shapes.

## Leaf Arrangement on the Twig

After determining the deciduous leaf shape, note how the leaves are arranged on the stem or twig. Trees with leaves that alternate on the stem or twig are shown first, followed by those that are directly opposite each other. Leaf shape and arrangement are shown in one icon for easy identification. Confirm your identification by examining the illustrations and reading the text for that tree.

### *Late Autumn and Winter Identification*

Between fall and leaf out, identification of deciduous trees will require examination of the form, bark, buds, and sometimes the fruit. The site where a tree is growing is a useful clue for naturally occurring trees. For example, silver maple, black gum, and pin oak, among others, grow naturally in wet sites. They also thrive when planted in upland sites, however. Use caution when identifying trees in town, in parks, or on a campus. Most will have been planted and the site will likely not be a useful guide. Becoming familiar with the bark, buds, and twig characteristics, which are consistent with tree species, is the reliable way to identify them when leaves are off. Bark is also a useful character in all seasons, especially when leaves are off.

# Coniferous and Deciduous Tree Groups Based on Leaf Type and Arrangement

## Conifers

Group 1. Needles in Bunches at the Ends of Short Spur Shoots

Group 2. Single Needles

Group 3. Needles in Bundles of Two

Group 4. Needles in Bundles of Three

Group 5. Needles in Bundles of Five

Group 6. Needles Scale-like or Flattened

## Broadleaf Trees

Group 7. Simple, Not Lobed, Alternate

# Conifers

## TAMARACK   Mélèze laricin

Eastern larch, hackmatack
*Larix laricina* (Du Roi) K. Koch
Pinaceae: Pine Family

**Size and Form.** Tamarack is a deciduous conifer with feathery, pale green needles that turn bright yellow in the fall. A medium-sized tree, up to 30 m tall and 30 to 60 cm in diameter; slender with a pyramidal crown. Branches slender and slightly ascending, major branches irregularly spaced along the trunk with smaller branches in between, making the crown appear ragged. In closed stands crowns are small, narrow, and conical.

**Leaves.** Needles are triangular in cross section, rounded above and ridged beneath, 2 to 5 cm long, blunt, stalkless, soft, flexible; borne singly on young twigs, in bunches of ten to twenty on short spur shoots on older branches. Leaves are pale green and deciduous. Autumn color: bright yellow, one of the last bright spots on the landscape in late autumn.

**Bark.** Thin and gray on young trees, becoming scaly and reddish brown with age.

**Twigs.** Slender, light orange-brown at first eventually turning dark brown. Leaf scars with one bundle trace. Spur branches are prominent with annual circles of leaf scars.

**Buds.** Small, lustrous, round, reddish, and nonresinous.

**Immature cones.** Appear in May through June with the leaves; monoecious. Pollen cones arise laterally on young twigs; borne in clusters; yellow when mature. Seed cones arise laterally on young twigs; oblong; red, pink, or yellowish green, on short stalks.

**Mature cones.** An oblong, blunt cone 1 to 2 cm long, light brown, on a stout, short, curved stalk. Ripening in the autumn of the first year, shedding its seeds during the fall and winter. Opened cones turn darker and persist for one to two years. Seeds are light brown, about 3 mm long, with a wing about 6 mm long.

**Distribution.** Found throughout western Connecticut, western Massachusetts, northern New England, and adjacent Canada. One of the most widely distributed North American conifers, occurs across Canada north to the limits of tree growth from Newfoundland and Labrador almost to Alaska with a major disjunct population in Alaska, in the northern United States from Minnesota to Maine.

**Habitat.** Found mainly on cold, wet, poorly drained sites, including swamps, sphagnum bogs, and stream and lakeshores. It grows faster and larger on moist, well-drained upland sites but is often quickly replaced by other trees on these sites. The most common associate in mixed stands on all sites is black spruce. In New England and adjacent Canada, other common associates include northern white-cedar, balsam fir, black ash, and red maple. A great variety of associated shrubs occur in the understory.

**Notes:** *Larix* from the Celtic word *lar* for "fat" in reference to the oily feel of the wood; *laricina*, "larch-like" because of its similarity to European larch. Tamarack is a very shade-intolerant pioneer species and the only native larch in eastern North America. Larch stands have been killed by periodic outbreaks of the larch sawfly (*Pristiphora erichsonii*). The wood is yellow to russet brown, medium to fine texture, with no distinct odor or taste. Now it is used primarily as pulpwood, formerly used for sills in ice houses and other outbuildings because of its resistance to decay. Once used extensively in shipbuilding for ship's knees, used to brace beams in wooden ships. They are cut from the natural curve where the trunk meets primary roots. That use continues today but at a much smaller scale. Tamarack has been planted as an ornamental. European larch, *Larix decidua* Mill., has been planted in New England both for forestry purposes because of its rapid early growth and as an ornamental. It has twigs that are stouter and yellowish, more and longer needles, and much larger cones with hairy scales. Japanese larch, *Larix leptolepsis* (Siebold and Zuccarini) Gordon, also has been planted in the region, but not as commonly as European larch. Its twigs are reddish, branches are longer, and cones are large with wavy scales.

### In the Field
- Irregular, almost ragged crown
- Feathery, light green needles borne in tufts on short spur branches
- Needles deciduous; turn bright yellow in fall
- Found on cold, wet sites

## BALSAM FIR    Sapin baumier

Balsam, Canadian balsam, eastern fir
*Abies balsamea* (L.) Mill.
Pinaceae: Pine family

**Size and Form.** Balsam fir is a medium-sized tree, up to 25 m high and 20 to 40 cm in diameter. In young, open-grown trees, the crown is pyramidal, open, and broad-based, consisting of slender, elongated, horizontal branches in distinct whorls of four to five, the lower branches sometimes slightly pendulous. In closed stands, dead branches persist below the live spire-like crown.

**Leaves.** Evergreen needles arranged spirally but appearing two-ranked on young growth, 1.3 to 3 cm long, spreading at right angles to the twig. Needles are stalkless, flat, blunt or slightly notched at the tip; dark green and shiny above, pale beneath due to white lines of pores; aromatic when crushed. Those near

the top of the crown are incurved, almost erect, entirely clothing the branches on the upper side, often sharp-pointed.

**Bark.** Thin and smooth on young trees, pale grayish brown, marked by raised resin blisters. On mature trees, the bark is pale reddish brown, separating into small, irregular, scaly plates.

**Twigs.** Slender, hairy, pale green, becoming red or yellow-green the first winter; later becoming light brown or purple-gray, smooth and somewhat shiny. Leaf scars distinctive, flush with surface, round. Pith white or tan, continuous.

**Buds.** Buds small, 3 to 6 mm long, clustered at the ends of twigs, globular to broadly egg-shaped, resinous, with shiny orange-green scales.

**Immature cones.** First appearing in May to June; monoecious. Pollen cones borne on the underside of lower crown branches in leaf axils, usually in dense clusters, yellowish red and tinged with purple, 3 mm long. Seed cones are borne on the upper side of the twigs in the topmost branches of the crown, singly or in small groups, purplish, about 2.5 cm long.

**Mature cones.** The seed cone matures the first fall; it is erect, oblong and cylindrical, finely hairy, dark purple, 5 to 10 cm long and 2.5 cm in diameter; resinous; scales are deciduous in fall leaving the erect cone axis, which can persist for many years. Seeds are winged and about 6 mm long.

**Distribution.** In New England, throughout most of Maine and New Hampshire, Vermont, western Massachusetts, and northwestern Connecticut. Widely distributed throughout New Brunswick and Quebec. In general from Newfoundland and Labrador west to Alberta southeast to southern Manitoba, Minnesota, east to New York, central Pennsylvania, and New England.

**Habitat.** A typical cold-climate tree that requires abundant moisture for best development. Associated tree species in New England and adjacent Canada include red spruce and to a lesser extent white and black spruce. Other conifers include northern white-cedar, eastern white pine, eastern hemlock, and tamarack. Commonly associated hardwoods include paper birch, yellow birch, quaking aspen, American beech, red maple, sugar maple, and mountain maple. Associated shrubs include beaked hazel (*Corylus cornuta* Marsh.), Labrador-tea (*Ledum groenlandicum* Oeder), Canada yew (*Taxus canadensis* Marsh.), red raspberry (*Rubus idaeus* L.), and hobblebush (*Viburnum lantanoides* Michx.). Herbaceous plants commonly associated with balsam fir are twinflower (*Linnaea borealis* L. subsp. *longiflora* Torr.), bunchberry (*Cornus canadensis* L.), starflower

(*Trientalis borealis* kaf.), creeping snowberry (*Gaultheria hispidula* (L.) Muhl. ex Bigelow), painted trillium (*Trillium undulatum* Wild.), false lily-of-the-valley (*Maianthemum canadense* Desf.), and spinulose wood-fern (*Dryopteris carthusiana* (Vill.) H.P. Fuchs).

**Notes:** The provincial tree of New Brunswick. *Abies* is the Latin name for an Old World species, and *balsamea* meaning balsamic, referring to the resinous bark blisters. The wood is creamy white to pale brown, light in weight, and soft. It is without distinctive odor or taste. The primary use is for pulpwood but it is also used for light-frame construction, paneling, and crates. Balsam fir is one of the most popular Christmas trees and greens are also widely used for wreath-making. Prolonged needle retention, color, and aromatic fragrance make it attractive for these uses. Dried needles and small twigs are used to make aromatic pillows. An oleoresin, commercially Canada balsam, is collected from bark blisters and used in microscopy and as cement in optical systems. The branches can be used to produce oil of balsam. Mature and over-mature trees are subject to periodic attacks by the spruce budworm (*Choristoneura fumiferana*). A closely related species, Fraser fir, *Abies fraseri* (Pursh) Poir., is found in the southern Appalachians in disjunct populations at high elevations in Virginia, North Carolina, and Tennessee. It is widely planted in this region as a Christmas tree and as an ornamental. Balsam fir provides food and cover for some mammals and birds. Moose rely on it as winter feed and white-tailed deer use it as cover and shelter during severe winter weather. Snowshoe hares use it for cover and red squirrels eat the seed. It is a part of the diet of spruce and ruffed grouse, especially in winter. Balsam fir is endangered in Connecticut.

### In the Field
- Pyramidal shape or spire-like crown
- Flat, stalkless, aromatic leaves and bark resin blisters
- Persistent erect cone axes

# EASTERN HEMLOCK   Pruche du Canada

Canada hemlock
*Tsuga canadensis* (L.) Carr.
Pinaceae: Pine Family

**Size and Form.** Eastern hemlock is a
medium-sized tree, up to 30 m tall and 60 to
100 cm in diameter. Young trees appear
exceedingly graceful with pyramidal form
and drooping branches. The crown is dense
and conical, and with age becomes ragged
and irregular. Branches are horizontal and
slender, drooping at the ends. The topmost growing tip is
flexible and curved, unlike any other northeastern conifer. The
lower branches tend to remain alive for many years, even in
dense stands, and dead branches persist. The trunk shows
considerable taper.

**Leaves.** Needles flat, spirally arranged and forming a flat spray
but appearing ranked, with a few tiny needles on top of twig,
stalked, 10 to 20 mm long, slightly tapered, edges with fine teeth
near tip, tip blunt, rounded, or notched; upper surface shiny,

dark yellowish green, two broad
white lines beneath on either side
of mid-vein. Needles become
progressively smaller toward the
tip of twig.

**Bark.** Scaly when young soon
developing wide flat ridges; on
mature trees becoming deeply
furrowed with dark brown
rounded ridges covered with thick
scales, inner bark layers purple.

**Twigs.** Slender; young growth yellowish brown and hairy,
eventually becoming grayish brown and hairless.

**Buds.** Egg-shaped, 2 mm long, slightly hairy, brownish.

**Immature cones.** First appearing in April to May, monoecious.

Pollen cones on branches of previous season's growth; light yellow at maturity, slightly globular clusters of pollen scales, 1 cm long. Seed cones at ends of new shoots, oblong, 3 mm long, pale green at time of pollination.

**Mature cones.** A small, egg-shaped cone, 12 to 20 mm long, on a short stalk; turning reddish or grayish brown in the fall. Margin of cone scales smooth or faintly toothed. Cones open in the fall and seeds are distributed throughout the winter into spring.

**Distribution.** Throughout New England (except southeastern Massachusetts) and adjacent Canada, prominent in the Maritimes. More generally from the Maritime Provinces, west through extreme southern Quebec and Ontario, southeastward into eastern Minnesota, Wisconsin, Michigan, New York, New England, and south through New Jersey, Pennsylvania, West Virginia, and Ohio, and in the Appalachian Mountains into northern Georgia. Many disjunct populations in some of these states and several others.

**Habitat.** Grows on a variety of soils but the best hemlock sites are universally characterized as moist to very moist with good drainage. Found along streams, shores of lakes and ponds, and along swamp borders. Eastern hemlock is a major component or common associate of several forest cover types and a minor component of many more. It occasionally occurs in pure stands but is most often associated with eastern white pine, red spruce, white spruce, red maple, and northern hardwoods (sugar maple, American beech, and yellow birch). Fully stocked stands of eastern hemlock form so dense a canopy that an understory seldom is able to develop. When an understory does develop, the most common herbs are false lily-of-the-valley (*Maianthemum canadense* Desf.), starflower (*Trientalis borealis* Raf.), wood-fern (*Dryopteris* spp.), common wood sorrel (*Oxalis montana* Raf.), goldthread (*Coptis trifolia* (L.) Salish), clubmoss species (*Lycopodium* L.), and sedge species (*Carex* L.). Common mosses are *Dicranum* and *Polytrichum*.

**Notes:** Eastern hemlock is a slow-growing, long-lived tree that is extremely shade-tolerant. It may take 250 to 300 years to reach maturity and may live for 800 years or more. It needs a cool, moist site to become established and can survive as a small tree in the shade of the understory for 100 years or more. Hemlock bark was once the source of tannin for the leather industry and many trees were harvested just for the bark. Today the bark is in high demand for landscape mulch; the wood is used for pulp and framing lumber. Because of inherent problems of shake (separation of wood along the annual rings) and difficulties in drying, the wood is relegated to the coarser grades of lumber. Groups and stands of mature hemlock are aesthetically attractive, hemlock is a food source for a number of wildlife species, provides nesting sites for some birds, cavities for hole nesting birds and denning mammals, and important winter shelter for ruffed grouse and white-tailed deer. It is also widely planted as an ornamental. Infestation by the hemlock woolly adelgid (*Adelges tsugae* Annand.), an exotic insect from Asia, is a serious threat to the future of hemlock. At present, the infestation front, moving from southern states north, is well established in southern New England and expected to continue northward.

### In the Field

- The terminal shoot is flexible and curved, unlike any other northeastern conifer
- Needles short, shiny, stalked, flat, and dark yellowish-green above, with whitish lines beneath
- Cones small, reddish to grayish brown
- Mature bark deeply furrowed with dark brown rounded ridges covered with thick scales; inner bark layers purple

## RED SPRUCE  Épinette rouge

Eastern spruce, he-balsam, yellow spruce
*Picea rubens* Sarg.
Pinaceae: Pine Family

**Size and Form.** Red spruce is a medium-sized tree, up to 25 m tall and 30 to 60 cm in diameter. The crown is narrowly conical and open. In the lower crown, slender spreading branches are horizontal or slightly downward sloping, and curve upward at the tips.

**Leaves.** Needles spirally arranged along shoot, standing out on all sides of the branches; stalked, curved inward, stiff, blunt-pointed but not sharp, four-sided; 10 to 16 mm long, yellowish green, and shiny. Crushed needles smell somewhat like orange rind.

**Bark.** Reddish brown, shredded on young trees; reddish black and separating into thin scales or plates on mature trees.

**Twigs.** Stout, reddish brown to orange-brown; short rusty or blackish hairs without glands. Becoming dark brown and smooth, eventually scaly.

**Buds.** Egg-shaped, 6 to 18 mm long, light brown, shiny or slightly resinous, outer scales fringed and narrow, projecting beyond end of bud.

**Immature cones.** First appearing in April to May; monoecious. Pollen cones bright red; young seed cones reddish green, in upper crown.

**Mature cones.** An ovate-oblong cone 3 to 5 cm long, blunt tipped, light reddish brown, pendent. Cone scales stiff with smooth or slightly notched margins; seeds dark brown, 2 mm long, wing 3 to 5 mm long. Cones ripen in fall of first year and seeds are dispersed; cones are shed the following year.

**Distribution.** The Maritime Provinces in Canada, southeastern Quebec, Maine, New Hampshire, Vermont, (primarily) western Massachusetts, and northwestern Connecticut. Unlike white spruce and black spruce, which are boreal species with transcontinental distributions, red spruce is limited to eastern North America and extends southerly in disjunct populations along the Appalachian Mountains to the southern United States.

**Habitat.** Grows best on well-drained, rocky upland soils and on the north side of mountain slopes in pure stands, but usually is mixed with other northern conifers and hardwoods. It is also found on wet sites. Associated trees on upland sites include balsam fir, eastern white pine, eastern hemlock, yellow birch, American beech, and sugar maple. On wet sites, it occurs with black spruce and tamarack. Because red spruce grows on a diversity of sites in various admixtures of tree species, the associated shrub and herb layer is variable. However, common shrubs include blueberries (*Vaccinium* spp.), witherod (*Viburnum nudum* L. var. *cassinoides* (L.) Torr. & Gray), speckled alder (*Alnus incana* ssp. *rugosa* (Du Roi), Clausen), beaked hazel (*Corylus cornuta* Marsh.), and hobblebush (*V. lantanoides* Michx.). The herb layer commonly includes bunchberry (*Cornus Canadensis* L.), wood sorrel (*Oxalis* spp.), twinflower (*Linnaea borealis* L. subsp. *longiflora* Torr.), starflower (*Trientalis borealis* Raf.), wild sarsaparilla (*Aralia nudicaulus* L.), and goldthread (*Coptis trifolia* (L.). Ground cover consists of mosses and lichens.

**Notes:** White, red, and black spruces are the three native spruces in eastern North America (see Notes for white spruce, page 16), and red spruce is the provincial tree of Nova Scotia. The wood is light in color, straight, even-grained, medium to fine textured, soft, and without characteristic odor or taste. Its major use in the United States and Canada is pulpwood. It is also used for framing lumber and in stringed musical instruments. Young red spruces in the northern forest understory are common nest sites of Swainson's thrushes.

- Needles stalked, four-sided; when crushed smell somewhat like orange rind
- Young twigs stout, reddish brown to orange-brown with short rusty or blackish hairs without glands
- Outer bud scales fringed and narrow, projecting beyond end of bud
- Cone scales stiff with smooth or slightly notched margins

# WHITE SPRUCE    Épinette blanche

Cat spruce, Canadian spruce, eastern spruce, skunk spruce
*Picea glauca* (Moench) Voss
Pinaceae: Pine Family

**Size and Form.** White spruce is a medium-
sized tree, up to 25 m tall and 30 to 60 cm in
diameter. The crown is broadly conical,
irregular, ragged, and rounded at the apex.
Long and thick primary branches are
horizontal or slightly downward sloping,
curving upward at the tips; densely clothed with stout pendant
lateral branches.

**Leaves.** Needles stalked, spirally arranged along shoot but those
on the lower side of the branches are turned upward so they all
appear to be crowded on the upper side; straight, stiff, pointed
but not sharp, square; 1 to 2 cm
long, pale blue-green at first
turning a dark blue-green.
Unpleasantly pungent when
crushed, suggestive of some of its
common names.

**Bark.** Smooth, thin, light gray. On
mature trees becoming darker
gray, separating into plate-like
scales.

**Twigs.** Light gray to yellowish brown, without hairs; smooth
except for persistent leaf bases.

**Buds.** Broadly egg-shaped, 3 to 6 mm long, light brown, scales
fringed, not projecting beyond the end of the bud.

**Immature cones.** First appearing May to June; monoecious.
Pollen cones red; young seed cones reddish, in upper crown.

**Mature cones.** An oblong cylindrical cone 3 to 6 cm long, blunt
tipped, light brown, pendent. Cone scales flexible with smooth

margins; seeds 2 to 4 mm long, wing 4 to 8 mm. Ripens in fall of first year, falls soon after dropping its seeds.

**Distribution.** In New England, found in most of Maine, northern New Hampshire and Vermont, and throughout adjacent Canada, and is widely planted for Christmas trees in southern New England. White spruce is a transcontinental species ranging from Newfoundland and Labrador west along the northern limit of trees through Alaska, almost to the Pacific Ocean.

**Habitat.** Common in the northern forest region, white spruce is able to grow on a diversity of sites. In northern New England and eastern Canada, it invades abandoned fields. Associated trees include black spruce, paper birch, quaking aspen, red spruce, and balsam fir. Undergrowth is characteristically sparse. Ground cover consists of mosses and lichens. As stands open up and light conditions improve, an understory of shrubs and herbs develops.

**Notes:** White, red, and black spruces are the three native spruces in eastern North America. Although there are physical differences among the three species, the odor of the crushed needles is perhaps the easiest way to tell them apart. White spruce emits the disagreeable odor of cat urine or skunk, red spruce smells like orange rind, and black spruce has a medicinal, menthol-like odor. The wood of white spruce is creamy white, straight, even-grained, medium to fine textured, soft, and without characteristic odor or taste. Its major use in the United States and Canada is pulpwood. It is also used for framing lumber, general millwork, paddles and oars, and musical instruments, such as piano sounding boards. White spruce is planted for forestry purposes and as an ornamental and Christmas tree.

> *In the Field*
> - Strong, disagreeable odor emitted from crushed needles
> - Twigs are without hairs
> - Cones are about 5 cm long with flexible scales
> - Bud scales are fringed, not projecting beyond the bud tip

# BLACK SPRUCE    Épinette noire

Bog spruce, swamp spruce
*Picea mariana* (Mill.) B.S.P.
Pinaceae: Pine Family

**Size and Form.** Black spruce is a small tree
on wet sites, up to 10 m tall and 30 cm in
diameter; on upland sites it is a medium-
sized tree, up to 30 m tall and 60 cm in
diameter. Crown spire-like, narrow, open,
and irregular. Branches are shorter than in
other spruces, downward sloping, curving upward at the tips.
Often branches in the upper crown curve upward, forming a
dense club-shaped top with many cones.

**Leaves.** Needles stalked, spirally arranged along the shoot,
standing out on all sides of the branches; slightly curved, stiff,
blunt-pointed but not sharp, four-sided; 8 to 15 mm long, dull
blue-green. Crushed needles have a medicinal or menthol smell.

**Bark.** Thin, scaly, reddish or
grayish brown; separating into
large, thin scales and becoming
darker with age.

**Twigs.** Yellowish brown to brown,
with short rusty or black hairs,
some tipped with a gland;
becoming dark brown, scaly, and
hairless.

**Buds.** Conical, blunt-tipped, 3 to 6 mm long, light reddish
brown, scales hairy with long slender points that project
beyond the end of the bud.

**Immature cone.** First appearing in May to early June;
monoecious. Pollen cones are produced in the upper crown
below the zone of female cones; seed cones are produced in the
upper crown.

**Mature cones.** An egg-shaped cone 2 to 4 cm long, purplish brown, pendent. Cone scales stiff and rigid, margins irregularly notched; seeds dark brown, 3 mm long, winged. Cones ripen in fall of first year, but slowly release seeds and remain on tree for up to 25 years with viable seed. Most seed is released within a few years; fire accelerates the rate of seed release.

**Distribution.** In New England, northern Connecticut, northwestern Rhode Island, Massachusetts (except southeastern Massachusetts), Maine, New Hampshire, Vermont, and adjacent Canada. Black spruce is a transcontinental species ranging west from Newfoundland and Labrador to Alaska almost to the Pacific coast.

**Habitat.** Typically found in sphagnum bogs, cold, springy swamps, and along streams but is also found on cool upland sites. Associated trees include tamarack, northern white-cedar, white spruce, and balsam fir. Dominant shrubs include beaked hazel (*Corylus cornuta* Marsh.), speckled alder (*Alnus incana* subsp. *rugosa* (Du Roi), Clausen), red osier (*Cornus sericea* L.), and red raspberry (*Rubus idaeus* L.). A few of the important associated herbs are fireweed (*Epilobium angustifolium* L.), twinflower (*Linnaea borealis* L. subsp. *longiflora* Torr.), wild sarsaparilla (*Aralia nudicaulus* L.), and starflower (*Trientalis borealis* Raf.). Ground cover consists of mosses.

**Notes:** White, red, and black spruces are the three native spruces in eastern North America (see Notes for white spruce, page 16). Besides regenerating by seed, black spruce regenerates by layering whereby lower branches become covered by mosses and young trees sprout around the tree, giving an appearance of a candelabra. The wood is similar to the other native spruces. Its major use in the United States and Canada is pulpwood. It is also used for framing lumber, general millwork, and musical instruments, such as piano sounding boards. Black spruce is the most commonly planted spruce for forestry purposes. Black spruce has been the source of some specialized products, such as healing salves from spruce gum, beverages from twigs and needles, aromatic distillations from needles, and binding tape from long split roots for birchbark canoes. Spruce grouse use black spruce stands for food and cover. Ruby-crowned kinglets, magnolia warblers, Cape May warblers, and ovenbirds nest and feed in black spruce stands.

Pine grosbeaks, pine siskins, and crossbills feed on black spruce seed. Red squirrels chew off the tips of cone-bearing branches, causing a club-shaped top.

> ### In the Field
> - Narrow crown, often with club-shaped top
> - Crushed needles have a medicinal or menthol smell
> - Young twigs yellowish brown to brown, with hairs tipped with glands
> - Bud scales hairy, pointed, projecting beyond the bud tip
> - Occurs on wetter sites than either red or white spruce
> - Cones smaller, more persistent than those of either red or white spruce

# NORWAY SPRUCE    Épicéa commun

*Picea abies* (L.) Karst.
Pinaceae: Pine Family

**Size and Form.** Norway spruce is a large tree, up to 40 m tall and 130 cm in diameter. The crown is dense, conical, spire-

topped, symmetrical, and very graceful. On mature trees, branches are upswept with vertically drooping branchlets; open grown trees have branches that persist nearly to the ground.

**Leaves.** Needles stalked spirally arranged along the shoot; straight, stiff, sharp-pointed, 12 to 24 mm long, dark-green.

**Bark.** Thin, reddish brown, wrinkled to smooth, or in small papery shreds. On mature trees becoming grayish brown or dark purplish brown and separated into small, hard, rounded scales.

**Twigs.** Light orange-brown, shiny, and hairless.

**Buds.** Conical, blunt pointed, reddish or orange brown, non-resinous, 5 to 10 mm long; bud scales sometimes with spreading tips.

**Immature cones.** Appear in May; monoecious. Pollen cones are yellow-brown in large groups in the upper crown. Seed cones are erect, purple.

**Mature cones.** A large, cylindrical cone, 10 to 18 cm long, rounded at the tip, light brown becoming reddish brown to grayish brown with age; lacking a stalk. Pendent from tips of branches in upper crown. Cone scales thin and stiff with finely toothed tips; seeds reddish brown, 4 mm with wing, 18 mm long. Ripens in fall of first year and drops in spring or summer of second year.

**Distribution.** Widely distributed in Europe and Asia, its native range, where it occurs on upland sites. Extensively planted in New England and adjacent Canada for forestry purposes, also widely planted as an ornamental.

**Habitat.** Grows well on a variety of soils; does best on mesic sites of acid, moist, fertile soils. Susceptible to drought and late frost. It rarely reproduces in the wild. Large trees found along forest roads, where its presence usually indicates a former house site.

**Notes:** Norway spruce is the major timber species in central Europe and is economically important throughout its native range. It is moderately shade-tolerant and fast growing. Many horticultural varieties have been developed. The wood is similar to that of native spruces, pale yellowish white, straight, even-grained, medium to fine textured, soft, and without characteristic odor or taste. Its major use in the United States and Canada is pulpwood. It is also used for framing lumber, general millwork, and musical instruments, such as piano sounding boards. Red squirrels commonly open the cones to eat the seeds.

> *In the Field*
> • Tips of primary branches are upswept, with long, droop-ing branchlets
> • Cones are much larger than those of native spruces

## BLUE SPRUCE    Épinette du Colorado

Colorado blue spruce, silver spruce
*Picea pungens* Engelm.
Pinaceae: Pine Family

**Size and Form.** Blue spruce is a medium-sized tree, up to 30 m
tall, 90 cm in diameter, slow growing and long-lived. It is native

to the central and southern
Rocky Mountains of the United
States, but because of its
attractive foliage and
symmetrical pyramidal form is
widely planted as an ornamental
throughout the United States,
Canada, and Europe.

**Leaves.** Needles are stalked and
spirally arranged, somewhat
upswept and curved forward; 15
to 25 mm long, stiff, very sharply pointed, square; new foliage
bright bluish gray or bluish green turning grayish green;
covered with a waxy bloom.

**Bark.** Purplish gray to brownish gray, loosely attached scales,
becoming red-brown and furrowed with age.

**Twigs.** Very stout, shiny, yellowish brown, hairless.

**Buds.** Rounded to blunt-pointed, 10 mm long; scales papery
and curving out in a rosette.

**Immature cones.** Pollen cones develop throughout the living
crown but are usually more abundant in the upper half of the
crown. The pollen cones are rose red but may appear yellowish
green on some trees. Seed cones develop in the upper 10 to 25
percent of the live crown, usually at the end of lateral branchlets.
Seed cones are initially pale green but turn red on most trees (on
some trees yellowish green), becoming pendent as they mature.

**Mature cones.** Cylindrical cones, 5 to 12 cm long, light brown,
scales thin, flexible, scale margin wavy and finely toothed.

**Distribution.** Extensively planted in New England and adjacent Canada as an ornamental.

**Habitat.** Grows well on a variety of soils, but does best on upland soils; is drought resistant. Shallow rooted on heavy or wet soils and susceptible to windthrow.

**Notes:** The species name *pungens* is from the Latin *pungere* meaning "to prick," referring to the sharp-pointed needles. At least thirty-eight cultivars of blue spruce have been named based on leaf coloration and crown form. Blue spruce is prized as a Christmas tree and is planted for that purpose. Mockingbirds commonly nest in residential trees.

*In the Field*
- Needles stiff, very sharp-pointed
- New foliage bright bluish gray or bluish green
- Found as a planted tree in New England and adjacent Canada, not a forest tree

# Group 3
## Needles in Bundles of Two

## JACK PINE    Pin gris

Banksian pine, Hudson Bay pine, scrub pine, gray pine
*Pinus banksiana* Lamb.
Pinaceae: Pine Family

**Size and Form.** Jack pine is a small to
medium-sized tree, up to 20 m tall, and 30
cm in diameter. Variable in form from
short, bushy, distorted, open-grown trees
on poor soils and rocky sites to trees with
tall straight trunks with little taper and a
short conical crown on better sites. Trees often appear scraggly,
branchy, and unkempt.

**Leaves.** Needles in bundles of
two, 2 to 3.5 cm long, yellowish
green at first, turning dark green,
straight and spread apart, slightly
twisted at the base, stiff, sharply
pointed, edges toothed. Sheath at
base of bundle short and
persistent.

**Bark.** Mature bark dark brown
with a slight tinge of red; divided
into irregular narrow, thick,
rounded scaly ridges.

**Twigs.** Slender, yellowish green at first, turning dark purplish
brown. Rough with persistent scales.

**Buds.** Terminal bud 6 mm long, egg-shaped, rounded at the tip,
pale reddish-brown, resinous. Lateral buds smaller.

**Immature cones.** First appearing in May and June, monoecious. Pollen cones in crowded clusters at the base of current year's branches, occurring in the mid- and lower crown, 1 to 2 cm long, yellow at maturity. Seed cones at the ends of branches in the upper crown, 0.6 cm long, in clusters of two to four. Dark purple at time of pollination.

**Mature cones.** The cones mature in autumn of the second year. They are variable in shape from oblong to conical, asymmetrical, resinous, 3 to 7 cm long, without a stalk; strongly curved, pointing toward the end of the branches. Cones remain closed for several years, persist on branches for ten or more years, and are covered with resin. They mostly open in response to heat from wildfire in the northern part of the range but in the southern part of the range may open in the absence of wildfire.

**Distribution.** Limited distribution in New England, mostly in central Maine and New Hampshire; in adjacent Canada, in the Maritime Provinces and western Gaspé. The major part of its range is in Canada, where it is the most widely distributed pine, occurring from Nova Scotia west to the Great Lakes States and north and west to the Mackenzie River in Northwest Territories.

**Habitat.** Jack pine can grow on very dry, sandy or gravelly soils, shallow soils, and rock outcrops, but grows best on well-drained loamy sand. Associated species in the northern forest are northern red oak, red pine, quaking aspen, paper birch, and balsam fir.

**Notes:** Jack pine is a fire-dependent species: fire opens the resin-bonded cones, kills competing vegetation, and prepares the ground for seed germination. It is a very shade-intolerant pioneer species; where fire frequency is low, it will gradually be replaced by more shade-tolerant species. Pure young jack pine stands in Michigan larger than 30 hectares are prime habitat for the Kirtland's warbler, an endangered species that breeds nowhere else in the world. Jack pine is used mostly for pulp. Its wood is unremarkable, and if sawn into lumber and timbers, is used for box lumber, pallets, and mine timbers.

**In the Field**
- Needles short, in pairs
- Needles are stiff, often twisted at the base, and spread apart from each other
- Cones variable in shape from oblong to conical, asymmetrical, resinous, strongly curved, erect

# SCOTS PINE    Pin sylvestre

Scotch pine
*Pinus sylvestris* L.
Pinaceae: Pine Family

**Size and Form.** Scots pine is the most widely distributed pine
in the world. It grows naturally from Scotland almost to the
Pacific Ocean and from above the Arctic Circle in Scandinavia

to the Mediterranean. It has been
planted widely in eastern North
America. It is a small tree in
North America, up to 18 m tall, 20
to 50 cm in diameter. There are
many genetic strains of this
species, some producing trees
with short, crooked stems and
wide crowns with many limbs,
and others with tall, straight
stems of good form.

**Leaves.** Needles in bundles of two, 5 to 7 cm long in a short,
persistent sheath; bluish green to grayish green; twisted, stiff,
sharply pointed. The needles slightly spread apart.

**Bark.** In the mid- to upper crown, the bark is distinctively
orange-brown, flaky or papery. On the lower stem it is
grayish- to reddish brown, deeply fissured into long, loose,
scaly plates.

**Twigs.** Twigs are slender, reddish to orange-brown, becoming
grayish brown; hairless and finely ribbed.

**Buds.** The buds are egg-shaped, sharp-pointed, reddish brown,
usually non-resinous, 6 to 12 mm long.

**Immature cones.** First appearing in late May to early June,
monoecious. Pollen cones tend to be concentrated on short
lateral twigs in the lower half of the crown, yellow when
mature. Seed cones are borne on the most vigorous shoots,
usually in the upper crown, reddish at time of pollination.

**Mature cones.** A conical to egg-shaped cone, often asymmetrical, 5 to 8 cm long; pendent, on a stout stalk, in clusters of two or three, pointing back along the stem. Scales are bright green at the beginning of the second season after pollination, becoming dull grayish brown at maturity that fall or winter; thickened at the tip into four-sided, recurved points. Seeds are released slowly from early winter to early spring.

**Distribution.** Widely planted throughout New England and adjacent Canada.

**Habitat.** Grows on any upland soil when planted but thrives on sandy loams; similar in habitat to red pine. In northern New York, where it has naturalized, associated trees are black cherry, red maple, sugar maple, American beech, quaking aspen, and eastern white pine.

**Notes:** Its Latin name means "pine of the woods." A shade-intolerant hard pine. Wood is similar to that of red pine and can be used for both pulpwood and sawlogs. Probably introduced to North America from Europe during the Colonial period. Widely planted as an ornamental, for Christmas trees, and for erosion control, occasionally for forestry purposes. It has become naturalized in some areas. Seed source is critical because characteristics of some geographic strains make them undesirable for certain uses on particular growing sites; it is susceptible to many pests and diseases.

---

### In the Field
- Needles twisted, in bundles of two, dull blue-green in color, sharply pointed
- Bark orange-brown
- Cones reflexed

# RED PINE   Pin rouge

Norway pine
*Pinus resinosa* Ait.
Pinaceae: Pine Family

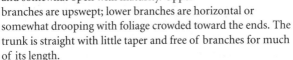

**Size and Form.** Red pine is a medium-sized tree, up to 25 m tall and 75 cm in diameter, occasionally larger. Trees 97 cm in diameter and 43 m tall in Michigan are among the largest living specimens. Crowns on young trees are conical, becoming broad, rounded, and somewhat open with maturity. Upper branches are upswept; lower branches are horizontal or somewhat drooping with foliage crowded toward the ends. The trunk is straight with little taper and free of branches for much of its length.

**Leaves.** Needles in bundles of two, 10 to 16 cm long, in a persistent sheath, shiny dark green, slender, straight, sharply pointed, and flexible but breaking cleanly when sharply bent.

**Bark.** Young bark orange-red and scaly. Mature bark thick and light reddish brown, broken into long, irregular diamond-shaped plates.

**Twigs.** Stout, rough with persistent scales, orange at first but becoming reddish brown.

**Buds.** Buds are 13 to 19 mm long, sharp-pointed, reddish brown, resinous, with rather loose, overlapping, hairy scales.

**Immature cones.** Appear in April to May, monoecious. Pollen cones, 10 to 20 mm long, purple, are clustered at the base of current year's branches, in the lower crown. The red seed cones, 2 to 4 mm long, are borne mostly in the middle third of the crown (in the upper third in older trees) at the ends of current year's branches, singly or in groups of two or three. Cones develop between the first and second year but actual fertilization does not take place until mid-July of the second year (thirteen months after pollination) when cone growth is completed and the fully developed seed coats have hardened.

**Mature cones.** Egg-shaped cones, 4 to 5 cm long, scales unarmed, borne on short stalks; ripening in fall of the second season. Seeds are released gradually from the time cones ripen throughout the following winter and into the next summer. The cones themselves usually fall the next spring or summer, although some may remain on the tree two or three years. The bases of fallen cones are concave.

**Distribution.** In New England and adjacent Canada, range extends from Cape Breton Island, Nova Scotia, Prince Edward Island, New Brunswick, southern Quebec, Maine, New Hampshire, and Vermont southward to northern and western Massachusetts and western Connecticut, and westward to central Ontario, southeastern Manitoba, and southeastern Minnesota.

**Habitat.** Occurs on dry, gravelly ridges, rock outcrops, sandy plains, and other sites where soil fertility is low. Usually found in small pure stands in northeastern North America or mixed with other species, most often eastern white pine, jack pine, quaking aspen, and bigtooth aspen. Where best growth occurs, in the upper Great Lakes Region, extensive pure stands occur. Red pine is shade-intolerant and fire-dependent for natural establishment.

**Notes:** Red pine is one of the most extensively planted trees in the northern United States and Canada, not only for wood production but also for control of wind erosion, windbreaks, and Christmas trees. Once widely planted around reservoirs. It is easily cultivated in nurseries and grown in plantations. The wood has an oily feel and a resinous odor, is moderately heavy, even-grained, pale reddish in color, and is used primarily for timber and pulpwood. It is easy to treat with preservatives, so it also is used for poles, pilings, and posts. The name Norway pine refers to its original discovery near Norway, Maine. An attractive tree in recreational areas, especially when the trees are large and located near a lake or stream.

*In the Field*

- Long, stiff needles more than 8 cm long, in twos that break cleanly when bent sharply (see Austrian pine, page 32)
- An egg-shaped cone, 4 to 5 cm long, scales unarmed, concave base
- Bark thick, reddish brown, broken into long, irregular diamond-shaped plates

## AUSTRIAN PINE   Pin noir d'Autriche

European black pine
*Pinus nigra* Arnold
Pinaceae: Pine Family

**Size and Form.** Austrian pine is a medium-sized tree, generally less than 30 m tall. A native of southern Europe, it is planted widely in North America as an ornamental, street tree, and in medians along highway systems because of its attractive dark green foliage and tolerance of salt spray, air pollution, and dry soils. The crown is broadly cone-shaped, with regular whorls of branches, becoming rounded at the top and irregular with age.

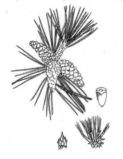

**Leaves.** Needles in bundles of two, 8 to 15 cm long, in a persistent sheath, dark green, slender, straight, sharply pointed, and stiff but not breaking cleanly when bent.

**Bark.** Dark brown or gray and deeply furrowed.

**Twigs.** Stout, yellowish green to greenish brown, hairless, rough.

**Buds.** Buds are about 1.5 cm long, sharp-pointed, pale brown, usually silvery-white, resinous, with rather loose, overlapping scales.

**Immature cones.** Appearing in May and June, monoecious. Pollen cones in clusters at the base of current year's branches, about 2 cm long, bright yellow at maturity. Seed cones at the tips of current year's branches, in clusters of one to five, bright red at time of pollination.

**Mature cones.** An egg-shaped, light brown cone, 5 to 8 cm long, scales armed with a sharp point, stalkless, erect, borne in clusters of 1 to 5, ripening in autumn of second year.

**Distribution.** Planted as an ornamental throughout the region, rarely found in the forest.

**Notes:** The word *Pinus* is from the Greek *pinos* for "pine tree," and *nigra* or "black" refers to the dark needles.

> *In the Field*
> - Long, stiff needles eight or more centimeters long, in twos, that do not break when bent sharply (see red pine, page 29)
> - Large cone persists on tree several years after seeds are dispersed
> - Bark dark brown or gray and deeply furrowed
> - Scale of seed cone armed with a prickle

# Group 4
## Needles in Bundles of Three

## PITCH PINE    Pin rigide

Black Norway pine
*Pinus rigida* Mill.
Pinaceae: Pine Family

**Size and Form.** Pitch pine is a small to
medium-sized tree, up to 20 m tall, 30 cm
in diameter. It is a tree of variable form;
shrub-like on the poorest sandy sites in
New England, on favorable sites a stout tree
with a straight trunk and an open, regular
crown. Trunks often have tufts of needles, some bearing cones.

**Leaves.** Needles in bundles of
three, 7 to 12 cm long, dark
yellowish green, stiff, twisted,
blunt, standing out at almost
right angles to the twig. Bundle
sheath persistent.

**Bark.** Mature bark dark reddish
brown, thick, divided by deep
furrows into broad flat-topped,
dark gray plates.

**Twigs.** Stout, greenish to orange turning dark grayish brown,
roughened by ridges and grooves.

**Buds.** Sharp-pointed, more or less oval or oblong, 1 to 2 cm
long; scales dark reddish brown, thin and fringed at the margin,
loose, often resinous.

**Immature cones.** First appearing in May to June, monoecious.
Pollen cones occur on lower branches in the crown, yellowish

when mature. Seed cones occur on branches higher up in the crown on the same tree, greenish with some red as maturing.

**Mature cones.** Narrowly egg-shaped cone when closed, egg-shaped and flattened at the base when opened, 5 to 10 cm long, usually at right angle to the branch, short-stalked; green turning light brown when mature. Scales thickened at the tip, armed with a rigid prickle. Ripening during the second season, cones open at maturity, at irregular intervals, or are opened by fire. Open cones remain on the tree up to a decade.

**Distribution.** Southern Maine and New Hampshire, the Connecticut River Valley and Champlain Valley in Vermont, throughout Massachusetts (except the Berkshire Hills), Connecticut, and Rhode Island. Rare in southern Quebec, along the Saint Lawrence River. More generally found in the mid-Atlantic States, west into Ohio and south in the Appalachian Mountains into Georgia.

**Habitat.** Usually restricted to less fertile sites, shallow or sandy or gravelly soils, on sandy outwash plains of glacial origin. In the highlands, it is most common on steep slopes, ridges, and plateaus. Grows on sites with a wide range of moisture conditions. It is the characteristic conifer on Cape Cod. Associated trees on drier sites include oaks, particularly bear or scrub oak (*Quercus ilicifolia* Wangenh.), and on wet sites, red maple and black gum. Eastern white pine often occurs with pitch pine. Lowbush blueberries (often *Vaccinium pallidum* Ait. or *V. angustifolium* Ait.), black huckleberry (*Gaylussacia baccata* (Wangenh.) K.) and dangleberry (*G. frondosa* (L.) Torr. & Gray ex Torr.) are common shrubs on drier sites; on wetter sites, a wide variety of shrubs occur, including sheep laurel (*Kalmia angustifolia* L.), highbush blueberry (*V. corymbosum* L.), and inkberry (*Ilex glabra* (L.) Gray) are common.

**Notes:** Pitch pine is slow growing and shade intolerant. It is a fire-adapted species that sprouts from dormant buds under the bark after a fire and has some cones that are opened by the heat of a fire. Fire usually kills competing vegetation and provides a suitable seedbed. The wood is similar to that of red pine but is of little commercial value in the northern part of its range. It is planted to reforest sandy sites and stabilize sand dunes.

Exclusion of fire and land development has greatly decreased the area occupied by pitch pine. Recent efforts have been made to perpetuate pitch pine with prescribed fire, for example on sand plains in New Hampshire, to maintain the habitat for a variety of plants, animals, and insects. Pitch pine seeds are eaten by many species of birds and small mammals, and many birds nest in the dense foliage, including mourning dove, brown thrasher, pine warbler, and purple finch.

**In the Field**
- Needles in bundles of three; pitch pine is the only native three-needled pine in northeastern North America
- Persistent cones with sharp spines
- Tufts of needles on trunk, some bearing cones

# Group 5
## Needles in Bundles of Five

## EASTERN WHITE PINE   Pin blanc

Northern white pine, Weymouth pine
*Pinus strobus* L.
Pinaceae: Pine Family

**Size and Form.** Eastern white pine is a
medium-sized to large tree, up to and
exceeding 30 m tall and 60 to 100 cm in
diameter; long-lived; fast growing. Young
trees have conical crowns with regular
whorls of branches. The crown in mature

trees is irregular with a few stout branches at nearly right angles
to the stem; upper branches ascend and often grow irregularly
away from the prevailing wind direction, giving the tree a flat-
topped, wind-swept appearance that is distinctive. In forest

stands, the crown is small and the
trunk with little taper is often free
of branches for two-thirds its
length.

**Leaves.** Needles in bundles of
five; 7 to 12 cm long; slender,
straight, three-sided, edges finely
toothed, flexible and soft; pale
blue-green; papery sheath at base
of bundle deciduous; needles
persistent about two years.

**Bark.** Thin, smooth, grayish green when young; with age
becoming thick (up to 5 cm), dark gray, and deeply fissured
longitudinally into broad scaly ridges.

**Twigs.** Slender, green, coated with rusty matted wooly hairs; later
smooth and light brown; finally thin, smooth, and greenish.

**Buds.** Slender, 6 to 15 mm long, sharp pointed, with many long-pointed, overlapping reddish brown scales.

**Immature cones.** First appearing in late May to early June, monoecious. Pollen cones clustered at the base of the season's growth, concentrated in mid-crown, oval and yellowish green at maturity. Seed cones in groups of one to five at tips of the season's growth in the upper crown, pinkish purple at time of pollination.

**Mature cones.** Cylindrical cone, 10 to 25 cm long, pendent, borne on a long stalk; green turning light brown when mature. Ripening during the second season, seeds fall during the autumn and winter. Opened cones fall during the winter and following spring. Scales slightly thickened at the tip, flexible. Fallen cones resinous.

**Distribution.** Found throughout New England (except outer Cape Cod and Nantucket, Massachusetts), and adjacent Canada. More generally from Newfoundland west across southern Canada into southeastern Manitoba, south in the United States from Minnesota east to Maine and south in the Appalachian Mountains into Georgia, with numerous disjunct populations in the Central States and along the eastern coast.

**Habitat.** Grows well on a wide variety of sites from dry sandy soils and rocky ridges to sphagnum bogs; grows best on well-drained sandy loam. White pine is a major component of several forest cover types and a component of two dozen more. It occurs in pure stands but most often it is associated with eastern hemlock, northern red oak and other oaks, red maple, hickories, aspens, red pine, and red spruce. The ground vegetation in a white pine stand varies greatly because it is a component in so many cover types.

**Notes:** White pine is one of the most valuable timber trees in eastern North America. It is the state tree of Maine and appears on the Maine state seal. In colonial times, white pine was used for houses, shipbuilding, furniture, containers, and most everything else made of wood. The Royal Navy claimed the tallest and best pines for ship masts, a point of contention between the colonies and England. But masts and large pine timbers became important items of trade for the colonies. The heartwood is light brown, sometimes with a reddish tinge, becoming darker with age. It has uniform texture, is easily worked with tools, straight grained, dimensionally stable, light in weight, and moderately soft, and has a pleasant piney odor. Most white pine is converted into lumber, where the better grades are used for patterns for castings, furniture, sash, doors, trim, paneling; lower grades are used in containers and packaging. Lower grade trees are used for pulpwood. Eastern white pine has a large number of insect pests and diseases, but the two that are most serious are white pine weevil (*Pissodes strobi*), causing deformity in the trunk especially on open-grown trees, and white pine blister rust (*Cronartium ribicola*), which can cause high mortality in young trees. White pine is widely planted as an ornamental and for forestry purposes, and is a popular Christmas tree. White pine provides food and nest sites for many birds, including early nesting robins and mourning doves, whose first nests are made before hardwoods leaf out. Decayed parts of white pines are excavated readily by woodpeckers for nest and roost holes.

*In the Field*
- The only five-needle pine native to eastern North America

## NORTHERN WHITE-CEDAR    Thuya occidental

Arborvitae, eastern white-cedar, swamp cedar
*Thuja occidentalis* L.
Cupressaceae: Cypress Family

**Size and Form.** Northern white-cedar is a
small tree, up to 15 m tall and 30 to 60 cm
in diameter. The crown is dense,
pyramidal, wide-based, often reaching the
ground. Branches bend slightly
downward before turning upward at the
tips. The trunk tapers rapidly, often leaning or twisted and
buttressed, irregular in cross section. Dead branches are
persistent on the lower trunk.

**Leaves.** Opposite, yellowish
green, scale-like needles, 3 to 6
mm long, not lustrous,
overlapping, glandular and pitted,
covering the twig. Needles on the
side of the twig are keeled, those
on the face are flat. Aromatic
when crushed.

**Bark.** Young bark thin and light
reddish brown; when mature it
breaks into long, narrow, flat
grayish strips, easily shredded.

**Twigs.** Slender, stiff, and usually horizontal. They are
yellowish green at first, flattened, broadly fan-shaped; turning
light red and eventually smooth, lustrous, and dark orange-
brown.

**Buds.** Naked and minute, covered by the last pair of scale-like leaves. Darkened tips at the end of some shoots look like buds but are preformed pollen or seed cones.

**Immature cones.** First appearing in April to May, monoecious. Pollen cones are borne singly at the ends of new shoots. They are tiny cone-like bodies, yellowish with black scales. Seed cones are also tiny, borne singly, at the end of new shoots; pinkish at time of pollination.

**Mature cones.** Appear the autumn of the first year and persist on the branch throughout winter. The cone is erect on a short stalk, pale brown, oval, small, 0.8 to 1.3 cm long, composed of eight to twelve scales.

**Distribution.** Found in scattered locations in all the southern New England states but extensively so in Maine, northern New Hampshire, and northern Vermont as well as western Nova Scotia, New Brunswick, and southern Quebec. Generally distributed from Anticosta Island and Nova Scotia westward to southern James Bay to southeastern Manitoba in Canada and the adjacent United States, and southward to Minnesota, Wisconsin, southern Michigan, and southern New York.

**Habitat.** Northern white-cedar is a tree of cool, moist, nutrient-rich sites such as organic soils near streams, rich swamps that have a strong flow of moderately mineral-rich water, or on calcium-rich mineral soils. It grows best on limestone-derived soils that are moist but well drained. However, most commercial stands are in nutrient-rich swamps, where they compete well with associated species. Northern white-cedar is sometimes found in pure stands but most often grows in association with balsam fir, black spruce, white spruce, red spruce, tamarack, black ash, and red maple on wetter sites. On better drained sites, associates include yellow birch, paper birch, quaking aspen, bigtooth aspen, balsam poplar, eastern hemlock, and eastern white pine. Common shrubs include speckled alder (*Alnus incana* (L.) Moench ssp. *rugosa* (Du Roi) Clausen) on the better sites and Labrador-tea (*Ledum groenlandicum* Oeder) and blueberries (*Vaccinium* spp.) on poorer sites. Sphagnum (*Sphagnum* spp.) and other mosses commonly cover the ground.

**Notes:** Northern white-cedar is shade tolerant and very slow growing, probably reaching an age of 400 years or more. It reproduces easily vegetatively, particularly in swamps where mature trees tip over and live branches come in contact with sphagnum ground cover. It is planted widely as a landscape tree (where it is commonly called arborvitae) either as individual trees or as a hedge. Many cultivars exist and are propagated from cuttings. The wood is light brown, has an aromatic spicy cedary odor, and is very resistant to decay. Uses include fencing and posts, cabin logs, lumber, poles, shingles, piling, boat building, and pulp wood. Northern white-cedar is highly preferred for winter shelter and browse by white-tailed deer, and is a common nest site of robins and house finches in residential areas.

*In the Field*
- Leaves scale-like, yellowish green, in four rows; flat-tened leaf-covered shoots
- Bark in long, narrow, flat, grayish strips, easily shredded
- Seed cones are small, oval, pale brown, composed of eight to twelve scales
- Crushed shoots are aromatic

# ATLANTIC WHITE-CEDAR

Southern white-cedar, white-cedar, swamp-cedar
*Chamaecyparis thyoides* (L.) B.S.P.
Cupressaceae: Cypress Family

**Size and Form.** Atlantic white-cedar is a
small tree in New England, up to 18 m tall
and 25 to 40 cm in diameter, but on good
sites in Virginia and North Carolina it
typically is 24 to 26 m in height. The crown
of forest trees is small, narrowly conical,
and is composed of slender limbs with somewhat drooping
branchlets. The trunk of mature trees in dense forest stands is
cylindrical and clear of branches for up to three-quarters of
its length.

**Leaves.** Scale-like needles 1.5 to 3
mm long, keeled and glandular
on the back, dark blue-green,
alternating in pairs at right
angles, overlapping, ovate,
turning brown the second year,
but persistent for several years.
Leaves on young shoots are awl-
shaped, spreading, without
glands, about 3 mm long.

**Bark.** Thin on young trees, 19 to 25 mm thick on mature trees,
ashy gray to reddish brown, somewhat similar in appearance to
that of northern white-cedar. It is fibrous with narrow
interconnecting ridges separated by shallow fissures.

**Twigs.** Branchlets are arrayed in fan-shaped sprays, at first
bluish green from the covering leaves, turning reddish brown
the first winter, eventually dark brown and slowly losing the
leaves, marked by scars of deciduous laterals, with small papery
scales.

**Buds.** Naked and minute, covered by the last pair of scale-like
leaves. Darkened tips at the end of some shoots look like buds
but are preformed pollen or seed cones.

**Needles Scale-like or Flattened**    43

**Immature cones.** First appearing in April to May, monoecious. Pollen cones are borne singly at the ends of new shoots. They are 3 mm long, oblong, four-sided with yellow pollen sacs. Seed cones are also terminal on different branches, usually solitary, 1.5 to 3 mm long, almost round, reddish brown at time of pollination.

**Mature cones.** A spherical cone about 6 mm in diameter, turning from a bluish purple to reddish brown, resembling a raisin. Cones mature at the end of the first growing season and are persistent on the twigs.

**Distribution.** In New England, Atlantic white-cedar grows in a narrow coastal belt from southern Maine to southern Connecticut. More generally found along the Atlantic coast from New York to North Carolina and the Gulf Coast along the Florida Panhandle into Alabama.

**Habitat.** Atlantic white-cedar is a tree of freshwater swamps and bogs, sometimes on sandy soils, but usually on peat or muck. Its range usually is restricted to coastal areas and to wet or swampy ground. Characteristically found in pure stands but associated trees may include red maple, eastern hemlock, eastern white pine, gray birch, and black gum.

**Notes:** *Chamaecyparis* is from the Greek meaning "dwarf" and *thyoides* meaning "like *Thuja*," a related genus containing northern white-cedar. Atlantic white-cedar is intermediate in shade tolerance, potentially a long-lived species although most stands rarely exceed 200 years. Atlantic white-cedar has a shallow root system and weak root hold in the spongy organic soils in which it grows and cannot withstand severe winds. The heartwood is light brown with a pinkish cast, a characteristic sweet cedary odor, and a faint bitter taste. It is light in weight, fine textured, straight grained, and is very resistant to decay. It is no longer considered of commercial importance in New England but still is harvested in the South. Uses include cooperage, wooden household furniture, boat building, fencing, posts, poles, pilings, and industrial millwork. It has limited wildlife value and is occasionally planted as an ornamental.

*In the Field*

- Leaves scale-like, dark blue-green, turning yellowish green in winter, in flat sprays
- Seed cones are spherical, about 6 mm in diameter, turning from a bluish purple to reddish brown, resembling a raisin
- Usually restricted to coastal areas and to freshwater swamps and bogs

# EASTERN REDCEDAR  Genévrier de Virgine

Red cedar, pencil cedar
*Juniperus virginiana* L.
Cupressaceae: Cypress Family

**Size and Form.** Eastern redcedar is a small
tree, up to 20 m tall and 30 to 60 cm in
diameter. The crown is narrowly
pyramidal or columnar, becoming open
and irregular with age; branches are short,
slender, and ascending. The trunk tapers
rapidly and is irregular in cross section,
fluted and buttressed in large older trees.

**Leaves.** Evergreen leaves are short
needles or scales, dark green to
bluish green and often covered
with a whitish bloom; they turn
yellowish brown in winter; on
young trees and newer growth on
older trees, needle-shaped leaves
are 12 to 19 mm long, arranged in
whorls; and, on older twigs and
trees, scale-like leaves are pointed,
2 mm long, opposite, compacted
to form a four-sided branchlet.

**Bark.** Thin, light reddish brown, fibrous, separating into long
narrow shreds; often ashy gray on exposed surfaces. Inner bark
brown and smooth.

**Twigs.** Slender, four-sided, green to reddish brown, smooth.

**Buds.** Buds are minute, inconspicuous, covered by the scale-
like leaves.

**Immature cones.** First appearing in April to May, usually
dioecious (rarely monoecious). Pollen cones are numerous,
minute, egg-shaped, yellowish at maturity. Seed cones are
solitary, small, egg-shaped, consisting of four to six fleshy,
bluish scales.

**Mature cones.** Berrylike cone, 3 to 6 mm in diameter, firm, dark blue and covered with a whitish bloom; ripening in the first season, usually containing one or two seeds, sometimes up to four.

**Distribution.** Found throughout southern New England, in the Champlain Valley, in the Connecticut River Valley in Vermont and New Hampshire, southern Maine, and into extreme southern Quebec. The most widely distributed conifer in the eastern United States., occurring in every state in the eastern half of the country; uncommon in Canada.

**Habitat.** Thrives on a wide variety of sites and soils from dry rock outcrops to wet swamps. It grows best on deep, moist, well-drained alluvial soils. Considered a pioneer species, it is among the first woody plants to invade old fields and abandoned pastures. Found growing along fence rows and roadsides. Associates include gray birch, red maple, black cherry, and aspens.

**Notes:** Shade-intolerant; drought resistant; very slow growing; long-lived (200 to 300 years). The heartwood is deep purplish red aging to reddish brown with characteristic "cedar chest" aroma. Redcedar is easily worked with tools and has straight grain. The heartwood is highly resistant to decay and insect attack. Once widely used in pencils, it has been replaced by incense-cedar (*Libocedrus decurrens* Torr.). Used for fence posts, chests, wardrobes, closet linings, carvings, pet bedding, furniture, flooring, scientific instruments, small boats, household and novelty items. It also is planted widely as an ornamental and is a popular Christmas tree. Oil extracted from the wood is used in the manufacture of perfumes and medicines. Cedar waxwings, robins, mockingbirds, bluebirds, ruffed grouse, wild turkeys, goldfinches, flickers, and grosbeaks eat the berry-like fruit. Birds play a large role in disseminating the seeds and seeds passed through their digestive tracts are much more likely to germinate. Sometimes a line of redcedars will be seen across a field or coastal dune, evidence that a fence or transmission wire was present at one time where birds perched and dropped seed. The dense foliage provides cover and protected nesting sites for robins, mockingbirds, cedar waxwings, cardinals, chipping sparrows, and flying squirrels.

### In the Field

- Foliage of two types: juvenile needle-shaped, 12 to 19 mm long, arranged in whorls; and scale-like on older twigs and trees
- Fruit berry-like, small, firm, dark blue with whitish bloom, resinous odor when crushed
- The bark is thin, light reddish brown, fibrous, separating into long narrow shreds

# Broadleaf
# Trees

## AMERICAN BASSWOOD   Tilleul d'Amérique

Basswood, American linden
*Tilia americana* L.
Tiliaceae: Linden Family

**Size and Form.** American basswood is a
large tree, up to 35 m tall and 91 to 122 cm
in diameter; reaching its best
development in the central Appalachians.
The trunk is straight, columnar, and free
of branches, extending into the upper
part of a symmetrical rounded crown,
consisting of spreading branches turned upward at the tips.
Open-grown trees have crowns with branches extending
almost to the ground.

**Leaves.** Deciduous, alternate, simple, and large; 12 to 15 cm
long and 7 to 10 cm wide. They are heart-shaped,

asymmetrical at the base, sharply
toothed, smooth, thick, dull dark
green above and paler
underneath. Autumn color:
yellow to orange.

**Bark.** Green to grayish green
and shiny on young trees; with
age becoming grayish brown
with narrow ridges and deep
furrows.

**Twigs.** Stout and somewhat zigzag, smooth, reddish
becoming yellowish brown, marked with scattered oblong
pores.

**Buds.** End bud and laterals are egg-shaped, pointed, asymmetrical, and divergent above the leaf scar; they are 5 to 7 mm long and reddish. Terminal bud absent.

**Flowers.** June to July after leaves appear. The fragrant, yellow-white perfect flowers are borne in pendulous loose clusters on long stalks attached to leaf-like bracts.

**Fruit.** A pea-sized nutlike drupe, usually containing one seed; gray-green and covered with brown hairs. Fruits are borne in clusters on a long stem attached to a characteristic persistent leaf-like bract that may remain on the tree into winter.

**Distribution.** Found throughout New England except for northern Maine. Also found in southwestern New Brunswick adjacent to eastern Maine and in southwestern Quebec adjacent to New Hampshire and Vermont. Generally distributed eastward through extreme southern Quebec, Ontario, and eastern Manitoba, and southward into adjacent states in the United States from extreme eastern North Dakota to Oklahoma and eastward to the Atlantic. In the Appalachian Mountains as far south as North Carolina and Tennessee.

**Habitat.** Basswood is found on loamy nutrient-rich soils in mixtures with other tree species, rarely in pure stands. It thrives in moist, well-drained bottomland soils and along streams and lakes. A common associate is sugar maple but it is also associated with beech, yellow birch, white ash, northern red oak, red maple, American elm, white pine, and hemlock.

**Notes:** The wood is creamy white to light brown with a faint but characteristic musty odor; soft and light, with a fine, even texture. It is used for lumber, veneer, plywood, furniture parts, pulp, woodenware, and novelties. It is a highly valued carving wood. Basswood flowers produce an abundance of nectar from which choice honey is made. In parts of its range, basswood is known as the bee-tree. Native Americans used the fibrous inner bark to make rope or for weaving. Basswood sprouts prolifically and may be found growing in a clump surrounding a stump. Basswood is an important ornamental but several European species are planted more frequently, particularly small-leaved linden (*Tilia cordata* Miller).

### In the Field
- Leaves alternate, simple, large, sharply toothed, and heart-shaped but asymmetrical at the base
- Bark grayish brown with narrow ridges and deep furrows
- Seeds borne in clusters on a long stem attached to a leaf-like bract that remains on the tree into winter
- End bud and laterals are reddish, ovate, pointed, asymmetrical, and divergent, 5 to 7 mm long

# EASTERN COTTONWOOD     Peuplier deltoïde

Eastern poplar
*Populus deltoides* Bart. Ex Marsh. subsp. *deltoides*
Salicaceae: Willow Family

**Size and Form.** Eastern cottonwood is a medium-sized tree, up to 30 m tall, 60 to 90 cm in diameter, but much larger where it grows best in the lower Mississippi River flood plain. The wide-spreading crown is rounded, open, and irregular, supported by a massive trunk that is often divided near the ground. In the forest, the trunk is long and straight, supporting a smaller, rounded crown.

**Leaves.** Deciduous, alternate, simple, 7.5 to 15 cm long, 10 to 13 cm wide, triangular, tapering to a sharp point, with coarse glandular teeth, base flat to heart-shaped, smooth and shiny dark green above, paler green and smooth below. Petiole slender, flattened, 4 to 8 cm long. Autumn color: yellow.

**Bark.** On young trees is light greenish yellow, eventually becoming ashy gray and is divided into thick, flattened or rounded ridges separated by deep fissures.

**Twigs.** Stout, angular, yellowish brown, smooth and angular in cross section; vigorous shoots have narrow linear ridges.

**Buds.** Terminal leaf bud is slender, angled, pointed, 12.5 to 19 mm long, yellowish brown, shiny, very resinous and fragrant. Lateral buds are similar but smaller, divergent; first scale on the lateral bud is centered directly above the leaf scar.

**Flowers.** April and May before the leaves appear; dioecious. Male flower in catkins 8 to 13 cm long, reddish. Female catkins are 15 to 30 cm long, with seed dispersed from June through mid-July.

**Fruit.** A capsule, egg-shaped, splitting into three or four parts, 6 to 12.5 mm long, smooth; seed is tiny, white or pale brown, and attached to a tuft of cottony white hair.

**Distribution.** In Vermont in the Champlain Valley extending into adjacent southern Quebec in the St. Lawrence River Valley, in the Connecticut River Valley in southern Vermont and New Hampshire, Massachusetts, and Connecticut, and the Housatonic River Valley in Connecticut. It is widespread in the Midwest, Plains states, and South where it achieves its best growth.

**Habitat.** Eastern cottonwood is found on moist, well-drained, fine sandy or silty loams close to streams and lakes. Associated trees include black willow, white ash, green ash, silver maple, red maple, American elm, and box elder.

**Notes:** The species name *deltoides* refers to the triangular leaf after the Greek letter *delta*. Eastern cottonwood is the fastest-growing commercial tree species in North America, short-lived and very shade intolerant. It is vegetatively propagated through stump sprouts and stem cuttings. The wood is soft and weak, grayish to light grayish brown, with a foul sour odor when wet but no characteristic odor or taste when dry. Today it primarily is used for pulpwood and interior furniture parts. Due to its rapid growth and ability to sprout from stumps, eastern cottonwood is considered a prime species for biomass plantations. White-tailed deer and rabbits browse eastern cottonwood seedlings and saplings and beaver frequently cut pole-size trees growing along watercourses.

> ### In the Field
> - Large triangular-shaped leaves with coarse teeth, lustrous shiny dark green above, paler green below
> - Buds are long, slender, angled, pointed, yellowish brown, shiny, very resinous and fragrant
> - Found in wet habitats along streams and lake shores

# BIGTOOTH ASPEN    Peuplier à grandes dents

Largetooth aspen, poplar, popple
*Populus grandidentata* Michx.
Saliaceae: Willow Family

**Size and Form.** Bigtooth aspen is a
medium-sized to large tree, up to 24 m tall
and 20 to 25 cm in diameter; it is fast
growing and short-lived. The trunk is
straight and columnar, supports a narrow,
open, round-topped crown, consisting of
slender rigid branches and stout twigs.

**Leaves.** Deciduous, alternate, nearly round to oval, 7 to 13 cm
long, 5 to 9 cm wide, pointed, coarsely and irregularly

toothed, smooth, somewhat
shiny green above, paler green
below. Petiole slender, somewhat
flattened, and long. Autumn
color: yellow.

**Bark.** Smooth, olive-green, with
maturity becoming brown and
furrowed, especially near the
base.

**Twigs.** Stout, smooth and shiny or with gray hairs, reddish to
yellowish brown, becoming gray and roughened.

**Buds.** Terminal leaf bud is egg-shaped, 7 to 8 mm long, dull
brown, finely hairy, not resinous or fragrant. Lateral buds are
more slender and smaller; a first scale of the lateral bud is
centered above the leaf scar.

**Flowers.** April to mid-May before the leaves appear, dioecious.
Male flowers in drooping catkins, 3 to 8 cm long, reddish.
Female catkins 3 to 8 cm long, hairy, scarlet; about 8 to 15 cm
long when mature; seeds dispersed within four weeks after
flowering.

**Fruit.** A capsule, narrowly cone-shaped, splitting into two

parts, 6 mm long, curved; seed is tiny, light brown, and
attached to a tuft of white hair.

**Distribution.** Found throughout New England and adjacent
Canada. Generally distributed from the Maritime Provinces
west across extreme southern Canada to southeastern
Manitoba and into the adjacent United States, south into Iowa
and east to the Atlantic coast.

**Habitat.** Bigtooth aspen grows on a wide variety of soils but is
less adaptable than quaking aspen. Grows well on sands or
sandy loams with shallow water table and does best on moist,
well-drained, sandy uplands with depth to water table no more
than 1.5 m. Common associates include quaking aspen, balsam
poplar, balsam fir, eastern white pine, white birch, red maple,
and red oak.

**Notes:** The species name, *grandidentata,* means large-
toothed. Bigtooth aspen is not as widely distributed as
quaking aspen. It is very shade-intolerant and is a pioneer
species on severely disturbed sites. When the parent stem dies
through cutting, fire, or browsing, extensive root suckering
occurs. Clones created by root suckers may be perpetuated
indefinitely by cutting or fire. The wood is light, soft, and
weak, creamy white to light grayish brown, without
characteristic odor and is not differentiated in the trade from
that of quaking aspen. Easily pulped by all commercial
processes, pulp being used for books, newsprint, and fine
printing papers. Used for fiberboard, panels (such as oriented
strand board), lumber, veneer, furniture parts, matchsticks,
and other small wooden products. Young aspen stands
provide preferred habitat for ruffed grouse. White-tailed
deer, moose, and eastern cottontails browse young aspen
stems and beaver cut them for food.

> ### In the Field
> - Leaves are nearly round to oval and coarsely and irreg-
>   ularly toothed
> - Leaf buds finely hairy, not resinous or fragrant
> - Bark smooth, olive-green, eventually becoming brown
>   and furrowed, especially near the base

# QUAKING ASPEN    Peuplier faux-tremble

Trembling aspen, golden aspen, trembling poplar
*Populus tremuloides* Michx.
Salicaceae: Willow Family

**Size and Form.** Quaking aspen is a
medium-sized tree, up to 25 m tall and 18
to 30 cm in diameter; it is fast growing and
short-lived. The trunk is normally straight
and supports a narrow, open, round-
topped crown, consisting of slender rigid
branches and stout twigs.

**Leaves.** Deciduous, alternate,
simple, nearly round, 4 to 8 cm in
diameter, sharply pointed, finely
toothed, smooth, somewhat shiny
green above, paler green below.
Petiole slender, distinctly
flattened, and 4 to 8 cm long.
Leaves tremble or quake with the
slightest breeze. Autumn color:
golden yellow.

**Bark.** Smooth, greenish white to cream-colored, becoming
furrowed, dark brown or gray, commonly roughened by warty
growths.

**Twigs.** Slender, shiny, reddish brown.

**Buds.** Terminal leaf bud is cone-shaped, angled, sharp pointed,
6 to 8 mm long, reddish brown, shiny, very slightly resinous but
not sticky or fragrant. Lateral buds are similar but smaller,
pressed against the shoot, tips curved inward; first scale of the
lateral bud is centered above the leaf scar.

**Flowers.** Mid-March to April before the leaves appear,
dioecious. Male flowers in catkins 4 to 8 cm long, reddish.
Female catkins are about 10 cm long when mature, hairy,
scarlet; seed dispersed within three to five weeks after ripening.

**Fruit.** A capsule, narrowly cone-shaped, splitting into two parts, 6 mm long, curved; seed is tiny, light brown, and attached to a tuft of white hair.

**Distribution.** Found throughout New England and adjacent Canada. Quaking aspen is the most widely distributed tree in North America, its range extending from Newfoundland and Labrador across Canada and into Alaska, south into the northern United States and throughout the western mountains into Mexico.

**Habitat.** Quaking aspen is one of the first tree species to colonize disturbed sites. It grows on a wide variety of soils but requires well-drained, nutrient-rich soils, and adequate moisture for best growth. Because of its wide distribution in North America, quaking aspen is associated with many tree species. Some of the more common in the East are balsam poplar, bigtooth aspen, white birch, white pine, red spruce, red maple, and red oak.

**Notes:** The species name *tremuloides* refers to the tendency of the leaves to tremble in the slightest breeze. Quaking aspen is very shade-intolerant. When the parent stem dies through cutting, fire, or browsing, extensive root suckering occurs. Clones created by root suckers may be perpetuated indefinitely by cutting or fire. The wood is light, soft, and weak, creamy white to light grayish brown, without characteristic odor. Easily pulped by all commercial processes, pulp being used for books, newsprint, and fine printing papers. Used for fiberboard, panels (such as oriented strand board), lumber, veneer, furniture parts, matchsticks and other small wooden products. Young aspen stands provide preferred habitat for ruffed grouse. White-tailed deer and eastern cottontails browse young aspen stems and beaver cut them for food. Baltimore orioles commonly nest in quaking aspens near water.

The genus *Populus* contains the aspens, cottonwoods, and poplars. Of the native species occurring in North America, the most commonly encountered in New England and adjacent Canada are quaking aspen, bigtooth aspen, and balsam poplar. Eastern cottonwood is widespread in the Midwest, Plains states, and in the southern United States but mostly restricted to major river valleys in southern New England and the Champlain Valley in Vermont and into southern Quebec in the Saint Lawrence River Valley. In addition to native species, several European species have been introduced, particularly white or silver poplar (*P. alba* L.) and Lombardy poplar (*P. nigra* var. *italica* Muenchh.). Several cultivars derived from the various species and their hybrids have frequently been planted. Natural hybrids also commonly occur making it difficult to identify species, even after observing flowers, fruits, and buds.

> ### In the Field
> - Bark smooth, greenish white to cream-colored, becoming roughened by warty growths
> - Nearly round leaves, sharply pointed, finely toothed, smooth, somewhat shiny green above, paler green below.
> - Leaf petiole slender and flattened, causing leaves to tremble with the slightest breeze
> - Buds cone-shaped, angled and sharp pointed, reddish brown, shiny, very slightly resinous but not sticky or fragrant

# BALSAM POPLAR   Peuplier baumier

Balm of Gilead, black cottonwood, tacamahac
*Populus balsamifera* L.
Salicaceae: Willow Family

**Size and Form.** Balsam poplar is a medium-sized tree, up to 25 m tall, 30 to 50 cm in diameter. Trunk is straight, with a narrow, open, irregular, rounded crown, supported by a few stout, ascending branches.

**Leaves.** Deciduous, alternate, simple, 7.5 to 15 cm long, 5 to 10 cm wide, egg-shaped at the base, tapering to a point, with many low rounded teeth, very dark green with orange or red veins above, silvery green, commonly with rusty brown, aromatic blotches below. Paired, warty glands common at the leaf base. Petiole circular in cross section and 7 to 10 cm long. Autumn color: yellow.

**Bark.** Greenish to reddish brown on young stems and limbs. With age, the bark becomes gray to grayish black and is divided into flat, scaly, or shaggy ridges separated by narrow fissures.

**Twigs.** Moderately stout, reddish brown to dark brown, shiny, with pores.

**Buds.** Terminal buds are broadly to narrowly cone-shaped, 12.5 to 25 mm long, reddish brown, very resinous, aromatic, and fragrant. Lateral buds smaller; first scale of lateral bud is centered above leaf scar.

**Flowers.** April and May before the leaves appear, dioecious. Male flower clusters or catkins are 5 to 9 cm long, reddish. Female catkins are 10 to 15 cm long and bright green turning dull green at time of seed dispersal from May through June.

**Fruit.** A light brown egg-shaped capsule, splitting into two parts, 6 mm long, smooth; seeds are tiny, pale brown, and attached to a tuft of long silky hair.

**Distribution.** Balsam poplar is distributed throughout most of Maine, northern New Hampshire, most of Vermont, and throughout adjacent Canada. It is the northernmost hardwood in North America, growing transcontinentally across Canada along the northern limit of trees. It is the largest tree in the northern part of its range.

**Habitat.** Grows in flood plains of river valleys, along stream banks, lake shores, and swamp borders. Prefers cool moist sites. In the East, usually found in mixed-species stands with white spruce, balsam fir, paper birch, black ash, American elm, red maple, tamarack, and northern white-cedar.

**Notes:** Balsam poplar is a boreal forest tree, a pioneer species that is hardy, fast growing, short-lived, and very shade-intolerant. It is propagated vegetatively through root suckers, stump sprouts, buried stems and branches, and stem cuttings. The wood is soft and weak, grayish to light grayish brown, with a foul sour odor when wet but no characteristic odor or taste when dry. Used for lumber, veneer, pulpwood, interior furniture parts, and woodenware. The balsam poplar hybrid *P. balsamifera* × *P. deltoide S* (*Populas* × *jackii* Sarg.) is planted as a windbreak in the plains. Other hybrids are being tested in short-rotation, intensively cultivated plantations. Ruffed grouse feed on male flower buds in winter. Moose and white-tailed deer browse balsam poplar stems and beaver frequently cut balsam poplar growing along watercourses. Native Americans recognized various extracts from winter buds as having therapeutic value.

### In the Field

- Large leaves with long tapering tip and many low, rounded teeth, very dark green with orange or red veins above, silvery green, commonly with rusty brown aromatic blotches below
- Warty glands at leaf base
- Leaf stalk long
- Terminal buds are long and pointed, reddish brown, very resinous, aromatic
- Found in wet habitats

# WEEPING WILLOW

*Salix babylonica* L.
Salicaceae: Willow Family

**Size and Form.** Weeping willow is a medium-sized to large tree, up to 25 m tall, 80 to 120 cm in diameter. The trunk is short and stout with a globe-shaped to oblong globe-shaped crown with

long slender drooping twigs that give the tree a weeping form.

**Leaves.** Deciduous, alternate, simple, 8 to 15 cm long, 1 to 1.5 cm wide. Leaves are narrowly lance-shaped, with a wedge-shaped base, margin finely sharply toothed, dark green and smooth above, paler below, glandless. Petiole short, glandular above, often hairy. Autumn color: yellow.

**Bark.** Mature bark gray and thick, ridged, fissured, light orange inner bark often visible.

**Twigs.** Slender, flexible, yellowish green, long, and pendulous.

**Buds.** Terminal bud absent; lateral buds are brownish, shiny, 2 to 5 mm long, one-scaled, narrow, sharply pointed, flattened.

**Flowers.** April to May with the leaves, dioecious. Male and female flowers in catkins 2 to 5 cm long, borne on short, leafy shoots.

**Fruit.** A pale brown, beaked, egg-shaped capsule, splitting into 2 parts, 6 mm long, smooth; seeds are tiny with a tuft of silky white hairs.

**Distribution.** Weeping willow is native to China, widely planted as an ornamental in Europe, North and South America.

**Habitat.** Weeping willow is very fast growing and grows best along river and stream banks, lake shores, and ponds. Planted specimens also thrive on upland sites.

**Notes:** Weeping willow is short-lived and very intolerant of shade but under proper light conditions on moist sites grows very fast. It is planted in city and suburban parks but does not make a good lawn tree because leaves, catkins, branches, and twigs litter the ground and an aggressive root system clogs drains. The tree is propagated easily from stem cuttings and a number of horticultural varieties have been developed. Male clones are usually cultivated. The tree is of no importance for wood products in North America.

> ### In the Field
> - Easily recognized by its long, slender, yellowish green, drooping twigs that normally reach the ground, giving the tree a weeping form

# BLACK WILLOW    Saule noir

Swamp willow
*Salix nigra* Marsh.
Salicaceae: Willow Family

**Size and Form.** Black willow is a small tree, up to 18 m tall, 15 to 46 cm in diameter in the northern part of its range. Trees are taller and of greater diameter in southern New England. It reaches its maximum development farther south. The trunk may be single but often forks at the base into two or more stems. Trunks are crooked and leaning. Stout spreading branches form a broadly rounded, irregular, open crown.

**Leaves.** Deciduous, alternate, simple, 7 to 15 cm long, 1 to 2 cm wide. Leaves are narrowly lance-shaped, often curved at the tip, with a rounded base, finely toothed margin, light green and somewhat shiny above, paler green below, glandless, with a short stem. Persistent, toothed, green, ear-like stipules at the base of the petiole.

**Bark.** Dark brown to nearly black, divided into deep fissures separating thick, interlacing, scaly, flat-topped ridges.

**Twigs.** Slender, reddish to orange-brown, flexible but brittle at the base.

**Buds.** Terminal bud is absent; lateral buds are reddish brown, shiny, 2 to 4 mm long, one-scaled, sharply pointed.

**Flowers.** May with the leaves, dioecious. Male and female flowers in erect catkins, 3 to 8 cm long, borne on short leafy shoots.

**Fruit.** Fruit is a light brown, egg-shaped capsule, splitting into two parts, 3 to 6 mm long, smooth; seeds are tiny with a tuft of silky white hairs.

**Distribution.** In New England, from southern Maine throughout the rest of the region, adjacent southern Quebec, and in New Brunswick along the south-central coast. Ranges west to southeastern Minnesota and south to southern Texas and northern Florida.

**Habitat.** Most of the thirty or so willows found in the northeastern United States occur as shrubs. Black willow is characteristic of river and stream banks, wet lake shores, freshwater marshes, swamp margins, and wet depressions. Often found as solitary trees, but commonly associated trees include eastern cottonwood, silver maple, red maple, green ash, and sycamore.

**Notes:** Black willow is the largest native willow in North America and is more distinctly a tree throughout its range than any other native willow. It is very intolerant of shade, fast growing, and short-lived. Needs moist conditions on mineral soil to germinate but can be propagated readily by cuttings and is used to stabilize banks of rivers and streams. At one time, the wood was used for making artificial limbs because of its lightness and interlocking grain but today is mainly used for low-value products such as pulpwood and fiberboard and low-value lumber.

Crack willow (*S. fragilis* L.), white willow (*S. alba* L.) and yellow stem willow (*S. alba* var. *vitellina* (L) Stokes), imported from Europe, have spread from cultivation and are found on moist soils along ponds and streams, wetland edges, forest edges, roadsides, and waste places throughout the region. Natural hybrids of crack and white willow commonly occur. Crack willow can be distinguished from black willow most readily by its whitish lower-leaf surface, small or absent stipules, gland-tipped irregularly toothed leaf margin, glands on the petiole near the leaf base, and a wedge-shaped or acute leaf base. Species identification may be difficult and require observation of flowers, fruit, and seeds in addition to leaf, twig, and bud characteristics.

### *In the Field*

- The trunk may be single but usually forks at the base into two or more crooked, leaning stems
- Bark is dark brown to nearly black, thick, deeply fissured
- Leaves are narrowly lance-shaped, often curved at the tip, with a rounded base
- Twigs are slender, reddish to orange-brown
- Found in very wet habitats

## COMMON APPLE    Paummier sauvage d'Europe

Apple, wild apple
*Malus pumila* (L.) Mill.
Rosaceae: Rose Family

**Size and Form.** Common apple is a small tree up to 12 m tall, and 60 cm in diameter. The trunk is short, dividing a few feet above the ground into wide-spreading stout branches supporting a broad, rounded crown. If not pruned, the crown often becomes irregular.

**Leaves.** Deciduous, alternate, simple, oval, 4 to 10 cm long, 3 to 6 cm wide. Leaves are sharply pointed, rounded, and asymmetrical at the base, margin irregularly toothed or smooth; at maturity, thick, dark dull green, hairless above, paler green with white downy hair below. Petiole stout and woolly. Autumn color: brown.

**Bark.** Thin, grayish brown, breaking into small, irregular scales, especially on the lower trunk.

**Twigs.** Moderately stout, hairy, becoming smooth, grayish brown, without thorns. Conspicuous fruit spurs short, stout, and rough.

**Buds.** Terminal bud is egg-shaped, blunt, hairy, grayish white, 3 to 6 mm long. Laterals are much smaller.

**Flowers.** May to June, when the leaves are about one-third grown, perfect, white or pinkish, 3 to 5 mm across, borne in clusters of several flowers on short shoots.

**Fruit.** A large pome (an apple), 3 to 8 cm wide, waxy green turning yellowish green to reddish yellow when ripe, persistent flower parts at top, brown seeds contained in a papery core. Flesh is edible but sour and often wormy.

**Distribution.** Native of southwestern Europe and western Asia but cultivated throughout Europe and in North America since colonial times. Escaped from cultivation and widely naturalized in eastern North America.

**Habitat.** Grows well on upland soils; found in second-growth forests, in old fields, along roads, on old home sites.

**Notes:** The species name *pumila* means small and refers to the small size of the cultivated tree. Common apple comprises the stock from which various varieties of cultivated apples have been derived. It is not a commercial timber species because of its small size and short trunk. The wood is hard, strong, close-grained, and reddish brown, used as firewood and, in the past, for tool handles. Moderately shade-tolerant and will persist but not thrive in the understory. If released from competition, provides a very valuable food source for wildlife. Besides the apples, porcupines eat the inner bark.

> ### In the Field
> - Short trunk, soon dividing into wide-spreading stout branches supporting a broad rounded crown
> - Leaves, twigs, and buds hairy
> - Flowers and fruit appear on short, stout spur shoots
> - Fruit large, yellowish green to reddish yellow when ripe

# DOWNY SERVICEBERRY    Amélanchier aborescent

Shadbush, Juneberry
*Amelanchier arborea* (Michx. f) Fern.
Rosaceae: Rose Family

**Size and Form.** Downy serviceberry is a
small tree, up to 10 m tall, 15 to 30 cm in
diameter. Trunk is long and slender; crown
narrow, rounded, and dense with many
small branches and slender twigs.

**Leaves.** Deciduous, alternate, simple, oblong, 5 to 10 cm long,
about half as wide, sharp-pointed, rounded at the base, margin
finely and sharply toothed with fewer than twenty-five teeth per
side, less than half as many veins. Leaves are softly hairy when

young, at maturity hairless and
dark green above, paler below
with hairy mid-rib and main
veins. Petiole slender, 1.5 to 3 cm
long. Autumn color: red.

**Bark.** Thin, smooth, gray,
divided by shallow fissures into
narrow, scaly, ridges on mature
trees.

**Twigs.** Slender, somewhat zigzag, smooth, light green,
becoming reddish brown. Pith star-shaped in cross section.

**Buds.** Terminal bud is narrow, 6 to 12 mm long, pointed,
greenish to purplish brown, twisted, hairy at the tip and along
the scale margins. Lateral buds similar, smaller, somewhat
divergent. Buds are similar to those of American beech except
smaller and with fewer scales. Leaf scars are very narrow.

**Flowers.** April to May when the leaves are small; perfect, large,
12 to 25 mm across, white, borne in erect or drooping, hairy
clusters, 8 to 10 cm long.

**Fruit.** A round, bright red pome, 0.8 to 1.2 cm in diameter, with
persistent flower parts at top, ripening in June or July and

turning dark purple with a slight bloom, borne on slender stems. The flesh is dry and tasteless. Seeds are numerous and small.

**Distribution.** Throughout New England and adjacent Canada in southern Ontario and Quebec. It ranges westward to Iowa and Missouri and southward to Louisiana and Georgia.

**Habitat.** Downy serviceberry is found in the forest understory, on dry, sandy sites, along forest edges, and rock outcrops. It is intolerant of wet soils. As an understory tree found in a variety of forest types, associated trees include white pine and oaks, hickories, sugar maple, American beech, and yellow birch.

**Notes:** Downy serviceberry is shade-tolerant, slow growing, and moderately long-lived. It is not a commercial timber species because of its small size. The wood is hard, heavy, strong, close-grained, dark brown with reddish shades. It is sometimes cut for fuel wood and in the past it was sometimes used for tool handles. It is planted as an ornamental because of its showy white flowers in early spring. In addition, two other serviceberries attain small-tree size in the region: Smooth Serviceberry (*A. laevis* Wieg.) and Roundleaf Serviceberry (*A. sanguinea* (Pursh) DC). Serviceberries are highly variable, and natural hybridization occurs, often making it difficult to identify species. Twigs, bark, and fruit provide food for many birds including phoebes, robins, wood thrushes, hermit thrushes, Swainson's thrushes, blackbirds, cedar waxwings, Baltimore orioles, cardinals, and rose-breasted grosbeaks, among others.

### In the Field
- Small tree with smooth, thin, gray bark, divided by shallow fissures into narrow, scaly ridges on mature trees
- Leaves oblong, sharp-pointed, finely, sharply toothed margin
- Buds long, narrow, sharp-pointed, twisted
- Showy white flowers
- Berry-like fruit, bright red turning dark purple

# PIN CHERRY    Cerisier de Pennsylvanie

Fire cherry, wild red cherry, bird cherry
*Prunus pensylvanica* L. f.
Rosaceae: Rose Family

**Size and Form.** Pin cherry is a small tree, up to 10 m tall, 15 to 25 cm in diameter. The trunk is slender, short, extending into the rounded crown. The open crown is narrow and rounded, with slender, ascending branches. On poor sites, pin cherry is a shrub.

**Leaves.** Deciduous, alternate, simple, lance-shaped, 8 to 11 cm long, gradually tapering to a sharp tip, margin finely and sharply toothed, with uneven, incurved teeth; thin and fragile; shiny yellow-green above, paler below, hairless; commonly curved backward. Autumn color: purplish red.

**Bark.** Mature bark is thin, smooth, reddish brown, with conspicuous horizontal orange lenticels; separating into thin, horizontal papery strips with age.

**Twigs.** Slender, hairless, bright red, with many pale pores, and often covered with a thin, grayish skin. Twigs have a bitter-almond odor and taste when crushed; pith brown.

**Buds.** Terminal buds are small, 1 to 2 mm long, round, blunt, reddish brown, smooth, clustered at the twig tip. Lateral buds similar, divergent and clustered near twig tip.

**Flowers.** May to June with the developing leaves, perfect, white, 12 to 16 mm broad with long stems; borne in clusters.

**Fruit.** A pea-shaped, bright red, one-seeded drupe about 5 to 7 mm in diameter, with an oblong, thin-walled pit, flesh thin and sour, borne on a long stalk.

**Simple, Not Lobed, Alternate    73**

**Distribution.** Found throughout New England and over a large portion of Canada from Newfoundland west to British Columbia, south to the lake states, and along the Appalachian Mountains to Georgia and Tennessee.

**Habitat.** Occurs after a heavy cutting or fire, but also along fence rows, roadsides, and other open disturbed areas. Associated trees include quaking aspen, bigtooth aspen, paper birch, yellow birch, striped maple, red maple, sugar maple, beech, northern red oak, balsam fir, and red spruce.

**Notes:** Pin cherry has no commercial value as a timber species but plays an important ecological role by quickly colonizing a site that has been cleared by cutting or fire. It is very fast growing, intolerant of shade, and short-lived, protecting the site from nutrient loss until other larger and more permanent species replace it. Several species of birds, especially thrushes, and mammals from mice to foxes and bears eat pin cherry fruit. Buds are eaten by ruffed grouse, foliage and twigs are browsed by white-tailed deer, moose, and hare. Distinguished from black cherry, which has reddish-brown hair on the underside of the leaf along the mid-rib; and from choke cherry, (*P. virginiana* L.), which is a shrub and has broader, almost egg-shaped leaves.

> ### In the Field
> - Leaves lance-shaped, margin finely and sharply toothed, with uneven, incurved teeth; thin and fragile; shiny yellow-green, hairless
> - Mature bark is thin, smooth, reddish brown, with conspicuous horizontal orange lenticels
> - Buds very small, divergent, and clustered near twig tip
> - Fruit, bright red cherries
> - Occurs as an early colonizer on disturbed sites

# BLACK CHERRY    Cerisier tardif

American cherry, wild black cherry, rum cherry, mountain
black cherry
*Prunus serotina* Ehrh.
Rosaceae: Rose Family

**Size and Form.** Black cherry is a medium-
sized tree, up to 20 m tall, 60 to 90 cm in
diameter. The trunk is long, straight, and
clear, with little taper and a narrow oblong
crown. The trunk of open-grown trees is
short, usually crooked, which continues into
an oblong, irregular crown.

**Leaves.** Deciduous, alternate, simple, 5 to 12 cm long, 2 to 4 cm
wide, lance shaped; gradually tapering to both ends, sharply

pointed, margin finely toothed,
teeth incurved. Leaves are dark
green and shiny above and paler
below, with reddish brown hair
along both sides of the mid-rib
near the leaf base. Petiole short,
slender with two red glands near
the leaf base. Autumn color:
yellow.

**Bark.** On young trees bark is
smooth, reddish brown to nearly
black, with conspicuous horizontal lenticels. On older trees, the
bark is nearly black, rough, and forms small, scaly, persisting
plates with upturned edges; lenticels still are visible.

**Twigs.** Slender, reddish brown, with many pale pores, and often
covered with a thin, gray skin that easily rubs off, with short
spur shoots on older growth. Twigs have a bitter-almond odor
and taste when crushed; pith white.

**Buds.** Terminal buds are 3 to 4 mm long, egg-shaped, blunt,
reddish brown, with several visible scales. Lateral buds are
similar but smaller. Bud scales are green near the base,
brownish in the upper half.

**Flowers.** May to June when leaves are nearly grown, perfect, white, 6 mm across, borne on slender stems in many-flowered clusters.

**Fruit.** A pea-shaped, one-seeded drupe about 10 mm in diameter, on a short stem, with a large, hard pit, almost black when ripe, flesh dark purple, borne in elongated drooping clusters of six to twelve fruits; ripen in August or early September.

**Distribution.** Found throughout New England except for northern Maine, adjacent southern New Brunswick, most of Nova Scotia, and southern Quebec adjacent to Vermont. Widespread throughout the eastern United States west to Minnesota and south to eastern Texas and central Florida. Absent from the lower Mississippi River Valley.

**Habitat.** Black cherry grows well on a wide variety of soils but grows best on rich, deep, moist soils where it occurs in mixture with other hardwoods. Associated trees are many and include oaks, hickories, basswood, yellow-poplar, white ash, red maple, sugar maple, beech, yellow birch, eastern white pine, hemlock, red spruce, and balsam fir. Associated shrubs include witch-hazel (*Hamamelis virginiana*), hobblebush (*Viburnum lantanoides*), and other viburnums (*V.* spp.).

**Notes:** *Prunus* is the ancient Latin name for plum and *serotina*, late, refers to later ripening fruit. Black cherry is the largest of the cherry trees occurring in eastern North America and the only one of commercial importance. Its wood is moderately heavy, hard, strong, straight-grained; the heartwood is light to dark cinnamon or reddish brown, with thin, yellowish sapwood. The wood has excellent working properties and its uses include fine furniture, cabinetry, veneer, interior finish, printing and engraving blocks, patterns for castings, piano actions, scientific instruments, and woodenware. It is the most valuable timber species in the eastern forest. The fruit is an important food source for many songbirds, squirrels, deer, wild turkeys, mice, and other small mammals.

### In the Field

- Leaves lance-shaped, with reddish brown hairs underneath along both sides of the mid-rib near the leaf base and two red glands also near the leaf base
- Mature bark is nearly black, rough, and forms small, scaly, persisting plates with upturned edges
- Fruit almost black in drooping clusters

# AMERICAN HOLLY    Houx d'Amérique

White holly, Christmas holly
*Ilex opaca* Ait.
Aquifoliaceae: Holly Family

**Size and Form.** American holly is a small
tree up to 9 m tall and 15 to 45 cm in
diameter. The trunk is straight and regular
but usually short. The crown is compact
and conical with slender spreading
horizontal or slightly drooping branches
often persisting to the ground. Branches
are covered in dark green evergreen leaves.

**Leaves.** Evergreen, alternate,
simple, elliptical, 5 to 10 cm long,
leathery, with or without lobes,
margin with distant spiny teeth.
Leaves are dark green, dull not
shiny, smooth, and centrally
grooved above, and have a short,
stout petiole.

**Bark.** Mature bark is grayish
white with numerous warty
growths.

**Twigs.** Stout, smooth, and pale brown.

**Buds.** Short, terminal sharply pointed, lateral buds blunt.

**Flowers.** June, dioecious. Borne singly or in a cluster of
flowers; male and female flowers are similar, with four to six
small, greenish white petals.

**Fruit.** The fruit, commonly called a berry, is actually a four-
seeded drupe. Fruits ripen from September to December and
remain on the tree through the winter. The fruit is round to
oblong, 6 to 12 cm in diameter, bright, but not shiny, red or
orange, occasionally yellow.

**Distribution.** In New England, spotty along the Atlantic coast from eastern and southeastern Massachusetts through Connecticut. A tree of the southeastern United States, it ranges southward along the Atlantic coastal plain from New Jersey to central Florida and westward to southeastern Missouri and eastern Texas.

**Habitat.** In the northeastern portion of its range, holly is found on sandy coastal soils or dry gravelly soils farther inland. It is tolerant of salt spray and it can be found growing along the coast in the protection of sand dunes. Associated trees include bear oak (*Quercus ilicifolia*), post oak, red maple, and pitch pine.

**Notes:** The genus name *Ilex,* from the Celtic *ac* (a point) referring to its armed leaves, and the species name *opaca* is in reference to the dull leaf surface, unlike the glossy leaves of the English holly. American holly is a very shade-tolerant, slow-growing tree. Sprays with berries were widely cut for Christmas decoration from wild trees. Today, cuttings from commercial holly orchards and artificial foliage largely satisfy that demand. American holly and numerous cultivars are widely planted as ornamentals throughout the region. American holly is not a commercially important timber species in the region, but where it grows best on deep moist bottomlands in the south (15 m in height, 60 cm in diameter), it is a timber tree of secondary importance. The heartwood of holly is ivory white with a bluish cast or streaks. The wood has no characteristic odor or taste and is heavy, hard, close-grained, and tough, with a low luster like ivory. The wood is difficult to work, but takes a high polish and it can be died black to look like ebony. It is used primarily for specialty items such as furniture and cabinet inlays, keys for musical instruments, scientific instruments, engravings, woodcuts, and carvings. Birds, especially thrushes, are the principal consumers of the fruit. Many species nest in American holly, including mockingbirds, catbirds, robins, and cardinals. Large winter-migrating flocks of cedar waxwings and American goldfinches consume large quantities of fruit and are important in seed dispersal.

**In the Field**
- Leaves evergreen, spine tipped, leathery
- Fruit bright red, orange, or occasionally yellow berries on female trees
- Naturally found in sandy, coastal habitats

# BLACK GUM    Nyssa sylvestre

Black tupelo, sour gum
*Nyssa sylvatica* Marsh.
Nyssaceae: Tupelo Family

**Size and Form.** Black gum is a medium-sized tree, normally 10 to 15 m tall, commonly found on wet sites: wet woods, wooded swamps, and bottomlands. The branching pattern is distinctive—the branches grow at right angles to the trunk, which extends well into the crown.

**Leaves.** Simple, alternate, 5 to 12 cm long, about half as wide, variable, from elliptical to long-oval; wedge-shaped at the base, abruptly pointed; smooth or wavy-margined, especially near the tip; thick, firm, hairless, dark green above, pale, sometimes hairy beneath; petiole short, reddish. Autumn color: bright or deep red, sometimes purplish.

**Bark.** Dark gray, brown, or reddish brown, deeply furrowed into long blocky ridges and tight thick plates.

**Twigs.** Slender, reddish or greenish brown, smooth, sometimes downy, becoming smooth and dark red-brown; pith white, diaphragmed, with dense greenish crossbars; short spur shoots often develop. Leaf scars broadly crescent-shaped, corky, with three sunken, whitish vein scars, no stipule scars.

**Buds.** Terminal bud dark red, turning bright red in spring, 3 to 6 mm long, oval, blunt-tipped with four or five scales, often hairy; lateral buds smaller, widely divergent.

**Flowers.** May to June when leaves are about half grown; inconspicuous, greenish white, on slender downy stalks, forming singly or in clusters. Male flowers in many-flowered heads. Female flowers sessile, in several-flowered clusters. Dioecious or sometimes polygamous dioecious.

**Fruit.** Small oval, blue-black drupe, 0.8 to 1.2 cm long, pit indistinctly ribbed; borne in clusters of one to three on a long stalk.

**Distribution.** Black gum occurs from southwestern Maine, southern New Hampshire, southern Vermont, and the Champlain Valley west to central Michigan and southernmost Ontario north of Lake Erie, south to east Texas and south-central Florida.

**Habitat.** Black gum grows best on moist, light-textured, rich silty alluvial soils, but also occurs on drier sites such as loamy lower slopes. In New England, it is most commonly associated with black ash–American elm–red maple forests, which occupy a range of poorly drained sites and riparian areas. In seasonally flooded backwaters, it is commonly associated with pin oak. Planted specimens do well on upland sites. Black gum is moderately shade-tolerant.

**Notes:** The name *Nyssa,* from Mount Nyssa in Turkey, legendary home of the water nymphs. The wood is heavy, soft yet very tough, pale yellow with thick, whitish sapwood and interlocking grain. It once was used for a variety of items that must withstand rough treatment: cable rollers and tool handles, factory flooring, and crates. The fruits are eaten by many birds including wood ducks, turkeys, thrushes and woodpeckers, and mammals such as black bear, foxes, raccoons, opossum, and squirrels; and it is an especially valuable den tree. An attractive ornamental, black gum is planted for its distinctive branching pattern, lustrous deep green summer foliage, and long-lasting red autumn color. Trees can reach great age; a New Hampshire specimen was found to be more than five hundred years old. Black gun is misnamed; it produces no gum.

### *In the Field*

- Leaves glossy with smooth margins, variable in shape, typically oval, broadest near the top, bright scarlet in autumn; leaves alternate on long shoots, in whorls on short shoots
- Branches thin, extending horizontally from an undivided trunk
- Bark thick, blocky
- Fruit a raisin-like drupe
- Naturally occurs on lowland sites with a high water table

## BLACK BIRCH    Bouleau flexible

Sweet birch, cherry birch (Canada)
*Betula lenta* L.
Betulaceae: Birch Family

**Size and Form.** Black birch is a small-sized
tree, up to 20 m tall, 30 to 60 cm in
diameter, with a long, tapering trunk,
rarely forked, with a narrow crown;
ascending or horizontal branches droop at
the tips. Rarely encountered as a specimen
tree or ornamental.

**Leaves.** Alternate, simple, oval to oblong-oval, 8 to 15 cm long
with slender, sharp-pointed tips; the base is unevenly heart-
shaped (occasionally rounded), with doubly toothed margins.
New leaves are light green and hairy, becoming dull darker
green and smooth above, light yellow-green with tufts of hair
in the angles of the veins beneath.
Few veins are forked. The petiole
is 2 to 2.5 cm long and hairy.
Autumn color: bright yellow.

**Bark.** Smooth, dark cherry red or
red-brown with conspicuous
horizontal lenticels on young
trees, becoming dark gray or black
and broken into irregular plates—
not peeling—with age. Somewhat
resembles bark of black cherry.

**Twigs.** New growth light green, sticky and hairy, becoming
orange-brown, shiny, and smooth with conspicuous pores in
summer and reddish brown by winter. When crushed, twigs
have a strong wintergreen flavor and odor.

**Buds.** Lustrous, mostly hairless, oval, pointed, light chestnut
brown, about 6 mm long diverging from the twig.

**Flowers.** Mid-April to May, monoecious. Male catkins form in
late summer or autumn, and open in the spring, before the

leaves; about 2 cm long, borne in drooping clusters at ends of twigs. Female catkins erect, borne terminally on short spur-like branches 1.3 to 2 cm long in leaf axils.

**Fruit.** An erect, oblong-oval, cone-like structure, 2.5 to 3.8 cm long, 1.3 cm in diameter on spur shoots, consisting of smooth, overlapping scales; containing winged nutlets. Seeds shed in autumn.

**Distribution.** In New England, black birch occurs primarily from southern Maine, central New Hampshire, and southern Vermont south throughout southern New England except absent from Cape Cod and the Islands. In Canada, limited to one confirmed location in southern Ontario at Port Dalhousie on the south shore of Lake Ontario. Black birch is primarily a tree of the northeastern United States, occurring south and west from New England through southern New York, northern New Jersey, Pennsylvania, and down the Appalachian Mountains to northern Georgia.

**Habitat.** Black birch grows best on moist, well-drained, fertile upland soils where it is commonly found with white ash, red oak, red maple, white pine, hemlock, yellow birch, sugar maple, beech, and white birch. It also occurs on dry, coarse-textured soils in association with eastern hemlock and black oak.

**Notes:** The word *Betula* is the classical Latin name of the birch, from its Celtic name *betu; lenta* means "supple" or "flexible," referring to the tough, flexible twigs. Black birch has light-colored sapwood and dark brown heartwood tinged with red, and is sold with yellow birch as birch lumber and veneer, the latter providing most of the supply. Uses are similar to those of yellow birch. Its wood darkens to a mahogany color when exposed to air and so was used formerly as an inexpensive substitute in furniture making. The tree was once the sole source of oil of wintergreen, but has been largely replaced by synthetics. Also, syrup was made from the sap in the same manner as maple syrup. Now black birch is a problem for southern New England foresters because it readily invades sites where red oak has been harvested, replacing that more commercially valuable tree; it also becomes dominant in eastern hemlock stands killed by the hemlock woolly adelgid.

### In the Field

- Leaves alternate on long shoots or paired on short shoots, light green, hairy when new, becoming yellow-green with tufts of hair in vein angles on underside
- Twigs smooth; when scraped have strong wintergreen taste and odor
- Bark cherry red on young stems, becoming dark gray-black and platy, not peeling, on mature trunks
- Fruit narrow, borne upright on twig

# YELLOW BIRCH     Bouleau jaune

Swamp birch
*Betula alleghaniensis* Britt.
Betulaceae: Birch Family

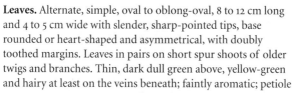

**Size and Form.** The largest of the native
birches, yellow birch is a medium-sized to
large tree up to 25 m in height and 100 cm
in diameter. The trunk is normally straight,
occasionally sinuous, with little taper.
Numerous slender drooping branches form
a broad, open, rounded crown. Trees can sometimes be found
on "stilt" roots in the forest, having developed from seed that
germinated on a rotted log or stump that has since disappeared.

**Leaves.** Alternate, simple, oval to oblong-oval, 8 to 12 cm long
and 4 to 5 cm wide with slender, sharp-pointed tips, base
rounded or heart-shaped and asymmetrical, with doubly
toothed margins. Leaves in pairs on short spur shoots of older
twigs and branches. Thin, dark dull green above, yellow-green
and hairy at least on the veins beneath; faintly aromatic; petiole
short, slender, grooved, and hairy.
Autumn color: dull yellow.

**Bark.** Thin, shiny, and red-brown
on young trees with conspicuous
horizontal lenticels, becoming
yellow-bronze with thin papery
scales with tight curls at the ends.
Old trunks becoming a dull dark
gray, irregularly fissured into large
thin plates, especially near the base.

**Twigs.** Slender, yellowish brown or brown, hairy when young,
with conspicuous pores, become smooth, shiny, and eventually
dull, dark brown, silver-gray or brown-orange; faint
wintergreen odor and taste.

**Buds.** Oval, sharp-pointed, 5 to 7 mm long, with three to five
bud scales, two shades of brown on each scale, hairy on the
margins; somewhat divergent. True terminal bud absent.

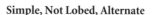

**Simple, Not Lobed, Alternate     87**

**Flowers.** April to May, monoecious. Male catkins are formed in late summer and mature the following spring, about 2 cm long in winter, 8 cm long at time of pollination. Female catkins oval, sessile, erect at pollination, 2 to 4 cm long, borne terminally on short, spurlike branches in leaf axils.

**Fruit.** An erect, oval, cone-like structure, 2.5 to 3.8 cm long, 1.8 cm in diameter, on spur shoots, consisting of smooth, overlapping scales, pubescent on the back; containing winged nutlets. In the north, heavy seedfall occurs after the first cold weather in October and continues through winter.

**Distribution.** Throughout New England except Cape Cod and the Islands, and adjacent Canada, generally from southeastern and southwestern Newfoundland, west through the Canadian Maritimes to southern Quebec and Ontario to extreme southeastern Manitoba, south to Minnesota, northern Illinois, Ohio, Pennsylvania, and northern New Jersey, and south in the Appalachian Mountains to northeastern Georgia.

**Habitat.** Characteristic of two types of forested sites: rich moist soils in northern hardwood forests, and poorly drained northern swamps. In northern hardwood forests it is commonly associated with sugar maple, beech, white ash, eastern hemlock, basswood, red maple, red oak, and white pine. In northern swamps, commonly associated with red maple, black spruce, black ash, and eastern hemlock. Also found along stream and lake margins. The most shade-tolerant of eastern birches.

**Notes:** *Alleghaniensis* means "of the Allegheny Mountains." Yellow birch, the provincial tree of Quebec, has white sapwood and light reddish brown heartwood and supplies most of the birch lumber and veneer. The wood is hard, heavy, and strong, with a fine uniform texture used in furniture, interior finish, doors, flooring, and woodenware. Veneer is used in plywood for flush doors, paneling, furniture, and cabinetry, especially figured veneer. The papery bark curls are very flammable even when wet. The catkins and buds are consumed readily by spruce and ruffed grouse; redpolls and pine siskins eat the seed.

### *In the Field*

- Leaves oval, more than a few veins branched; alternate on long shoots, paired on short spur shoots on older branches
- Bud scales with two shades of brown, hairy margins
- Young twigs hairy; twigs with a slight wintergreen smell and flavor when scraped
- Bark initially bronze, turning yellow-gray with tight curls broken into irregular plates on large trees
- Fruit cone-like, borne upright on twig

# RIVER BIRCH

Red birch, water birch
*Betula nigra* L.
Betulaceae: Birch Family

**Size and Form.** River birch is a small to medium-sized tree, up to 25 m tall, with either a single trunk or trunk divided into two or more strictly upright branches with a narrow, round-topped, open, irregular crown. The lateral branches are slender and horizontal, sometimes drooping.

**Leaves.** Alternate, simple, broadly oval and pointed, wedge-shaped at the base, with doubly toothed margins, 4 to 7.5 cm long; six to ten pairs of prominent veins; more or less hairy on both surfaces when young, when mature dark-green, shiny, smooth above, pale yellowish green below, petiole slender, hairy, about 1.3 cm long. Autumn color: dull yellow.

**Bark.** On young trunks and on the upper part of mature trunks and on the branches, bark is light brown to red-brown, peeling in thin, papery, clinging scales; at the base of mature trunks, dark brown and more or less deeply fissured.

**Twigs.** Slender, hairy when young, smooth and reddish brown with dark dots by the first winter.

**Buds.** Oval with a pointed tip, smooth or somewhat hairy, reddish brown, about 10 mm long, somewhat divergent.

**Flowers.** March to April, before the leaves, monoecious. Male catkins are formed in clusters in late summer at twig tips, mature the following spring, becoming 5 to 7.5 cm long. Female catkins much shorter, about 8 mm long, solitary at the tips of short, two-leaved spur-shoots.

**Fruit.** An erect, pale brown, oblong-oval, cone-like structure, 2.5 to 4 cm long, 1.3 centimeters in diameter, consisting of overlapping scales, pubescent on the back; containing winged nutlets. Mature in May or June and shed seeds in mid-summer. Unlike most other birches, the seed germinates immediately upon falling.

**Distribution.** In New England, southeastern New Hampshire, the Merrimack River Valley in Massachusetts, several locations in north-central and southwestern Connecticut. Elsewhere, largely a tree of the southeastern United States, primarily from Virginia west to Iowa, and south to east Texas and northern Florida.

**Habitat.** Naturally occurs on alluvial soils along stream or river banks and bottoms where the soil is saturated year-round, although it doesn't tolerate flooding and is absent from much of the Mississippi River floodplain. It is frequently planted as an ornamental on a variety of drier sites.

**Notes:** The word *nigra* is Latin for "black"; river birch was the first of the dark-barked birches to be named. The wood is of little commercial importance partly because of its poor form, but similar in characteristics to other birches. The twigs once were used to make birch brooms. It is planted as an ornamental because of its graceful form, attractive bark, and because it has no serious insect pests. The largest recorded river birch in Massachusetts is in Concord: 84 cm in diameter and 20 m tall with a 17-m crown spread.

> ### *In the Field*
> - Leaves almost diamond-shaped, doubly toothed, wedged-shaped at the base, some leaves on new shoots have teeth resembling shallow lobes
> - Bark ragged, peeling in thin, tight, clinging papery ridges. Cinnamon, white, and brown hues
> - Naturally found near water

## PAPER BIRCH    Bouleau à papier

White birch, canoe birch
*Betula papyrifera* Marsh.
Betulaceae: Birch Family

**Size and Form.** Paper birch is a small to
medium-sized tree, up to 25 m tall and 60
cm in diameter, readily recognized by its
white bark. Young trees have a cone-
shaped or oval crown of many slender
branches ending in very fine twigs. In
older trees the trunk is long and branchless, sometimes curved
or leaning, with an open crown formed by a few large upright
limbs with a few horizontal branches.

**Leaves.** Alternate, simple, solitary
on long shoots, in threes on short
spur shoots of older branches;
oval or triangular, 5 to 10 cm long
with a pointed tip and the base
wedge-shaped, rounded, or
obtuse (heart-shaped in the
variety *cordifolia*), margins doubly
toothed; dull dark green above,
paler beneath; with minute black
glands, nine or fewer paired veins,
each vein ending in a large tooth, with three to five intervening
smaller teeth. Petioles yellow and stout, with black glands,
smooth or somewhat hairy. Autumn color: yellow.

**Bark.** On young trees thin, smooth, and reddish brown,
becoming cream colored or white on the trunk and large
branches; inner bark orange. Outer bark separates into thin
papery peels or sheets; furrowed and blackish at the base.
Horizontal lenticels are conspicuous. Where the white bark is
removed the inner orange bark dies, turns black, and divides into
flakes. Removing large areas of the outer bark may kill the tree.

**Twigs.** Slender, dull red, and hairy during the first weeks of
growth, becoming dark reddish brown and smooth, and finally
gray with sparse resin glands.

**Buds.** Oval, slender, blunt-pointed, 5 to 7 mm long, three to five scales green toward base, brown toward tip, somewhat flattened, sticky, divergent. True terminal bud absent.

**Flowers.** April to May, before or with the leaves, monoecious. Male catkins single or in clusters of two to three are formed in late summer and maturing the following spring, about 9 cm long, pendent and brownish at pollination, borne at the end of twigs and lateral shoots. Female catkins greenish, 2.5 to 5 cm long, erect, on spur shoots.

**Fruit.** A pendent, cylindrical, long-stalked, pale brown, cone-like structure, 3 to 4 cm long, 1 cm in diameter, consisting of smooth or minutely pubescent, overlapping scales; containing winged nutlets, shed rapidly when ripe in August to September.

**Distribution.** Throughout northern New England and adjacent Canada south through most of Massachusetts, northern Connecticut, and Rhode Island. Elsewhere, the northern limit of paper birch closely follows the northern limit of tree growth from Newfoundland, Labrador, and the Maritimes west across the continent to northwestern Alaska, and south to the northern Rocky Mountains with scattered populations across the northern Great Plains and throughout the Lake States.

**Habitat.** In New England, paper birch tends to be more abundant on dry sites than on wet or poorly drained soils, although throughout its range it occurs on a wide variety of sites. Commonly found growing in pure stands following fire or clearcutting, it also grows on forest edges, lakeshores, roadsides, and is a common member of all northern forest types including northern hardwoods, and spruce-fir. It is not shade-tolerant and is often the first tree to reforest areas that have been burned or cut.

**Notes:** *Papyrifera* means "paper bearing," from the Greek *papyrus* (paper) and the Latin *ferre* (to bear), referring to the white, papery bark. Very fast-growing, shade-intolerant, and short lived. Native Americans used the bark for canoes, wigwam coverings, and utensils. The wood is light, strong, hard, with a fine, uniform texture, light reddish brown with nearly white sapwood. Largely used in turned products such as spools, small handles, and toys; also chipped for pulp wood and fuel wood. Often planted as an ornamental, but highly susceptible to the bronze birch borer (*Agrilus anxius*). Ruffed grouse eat the buds and catkins and many small northern forest birds and mice consume the seed. Isolated trees left after forest clearing usually die. Paper birch is the state tree of New Hampshire.

*In the Field*
- Leaves rounded at the base, widest below the middle; leaves on spur shoots in threes
- Bark white and papery when mature, peeling in large, thin sheets
- Bud scales green and brown
- Fruit bracts cross-shaped, middle lobe short and pointed
- Catkins in twos or threes
- Nutlet with wide wings
- Twigs have no wintergreen taste or odor when scraped
- Typically a single trunk in the wild

## GRAY BIRCH   Bouleau gris

Poverty birch, old-field birch, wire birch
*Betula populifolia* Marsh.
Betulaceae: Birch Family

**Size and Form.** A small tree, rarely
exceeding 10 m in height, 15 to 30 cm in
diameter. Gray birch is a northeastern tree
that invades old fields and burns. It normally
has two to six leaning trunks arising from a
common root-crown; trunks are distinct to
nearly the top of the open, irregular, narrow
pyramid-shaped crown; retains its dead lower branches.

**Leaves.** Alternate, simple, and triangular, 4 to 6 cm long, with a
long-pointed tapering tip, base almost straight, leaves hang
down on slender stems; upper surface rough-textured and shiny
dark green, shiny and lighter green beneath; six to nine paired
veins, each ending in a large lobe-like tooth, with smaller
intervening teeth. Preformed leaves hairless, dwarf leaves

somewhat hairy. Autumn color:
yellow-brown.

**Bark.** Thin, smooth, chestnut
brown on young stems, becoming
dull chalky-white; broad black
chevron patches commonly form
just below the branches, caused by
a fungus (*Pseudospiropes
longipilus*) growing on resinous
excretions from the bark.

**Twigs.** Slender, gray or gray-brown, hairless, with numerous
resin glands; tips of twigs have a sandpapery texture.

**Buds.** Pointed, divergent from the twig, uniformly light brown-
gray, somewhat resinous, often hairy.

**Flowers.** Late March to April, with the leaves, monoecious.
Male catkins are formed in late summer and mature the
following spring, normally solitary, about 2 cm long in winter,

**Simple, Not Lobed, Alternate   95**

6 to 10 cm at pollination. Female catkins 1 to 1.5 cm long, solitary at the tips of short, two-leaved spur-shoots.

**Fruit.** A semi-erect, pale brown, cylindrical, cone-like structure, 1.5 to 2 cm long, narrow, blunt-tipped, consisting of overlapping scales, minutely hairy; containing winged nutlets. Shed in late autumn or early winter.

**Distribution.** Except in northernmost Maine, gray birch occurs throughout New England, which is the center of its range, and adjacent Canada. The overall range extends from Prince Edward Island and southern Nova Scotia, southern Quebec, and southeastern Ontario, south through northern and eastern New York, eastern Pennsylvania, and New Jersey south to North Carolina.

**Habitat.** Gray birch occurs on sandy or gravelly soils irrespective of moisture regime. It is a rapid invader of abandoned fields and pastures, sites where the soils have been disturbed or removed, and recently burned areas where it commonly forms almost pure stands. On very poor sites, it commonly is associated with sweetfern (*Comptonia peregrina* (L.) Coult.) and little bluestem *(Schizachyrium scoparius* (Michx.) Nash). It is shade-intolerant, short-lived, and soon replaced by more shade-tolerant and longer-lived species.

**Notes:** *Populifolia* means with leaves like poplar. Leafs out about one week later than white birch. May be extending its range northward and westward, colonizing abandoned farmland. Many small birds and mammals consume the seed.

> ### In the Field
> - Leaf triangular with flat base and long, tapering pointed tip
> - Chalky white nonpeeling bark with black chevron patches immediately below the branches; dead lower branches retained
> - Catkins usually borne singly
> - Twigs covered with crusty pores, sandpapery toward tips
> - Usually with multiple trunks in the wild

# AMERICAN HORNBEAM    Charme de Caroline

Blue-beech, musclewood, ironwood
*Carpinus caroliniana* Walt. ssp. *virginiana* (Marsh.) Furlow
Betulaceae: Birch Family

**Size and Form.** American hornbeam is a very
small tree or large shrub, 3 to 8 m (rarely
more) tall and 15 to 30 cm in diameter. The
trunk is short, crooked or twisted, and
leaning, with vertical, muscle-like ridges. The
branches are slender and zigzag with fine
twigs in flat sprays forming a low, wide, flat-topped crown.

**Leaves.** Alternate, simple, 5 to 10
cm long, oval and long-pointed,
arranged in two rows on the twig;
sharply doubly toothed with larger
teeth at the ends of the larger
veins; thin, firm, dull blue-green
above; lighter beneath; petiole
short, slender, and hairy. Autumn
color: deep red or orange.

**Bark.** Thin, smooth, slate gray,
and unbroken.

**Twigs.** Slender, new growth pale green and hairy, as narrow as
the leaf buds, becoming gray to red-brown and smooth by the
first winter.

**Buds.** End and lateral buds 3 mm long, long-oval and blunt,
slightly hairy, pressed against the twig, scales in four rows,
reddish brown with white margins. True terminal bud absent.
Leaf scar with three vein scars.

**Flowers.** April to May, with the leaves, monoecious. Male
flowers (not visible until spring, unlike the true birches) in
drooping catkins 2.5 to 4 cm long at pollination, borne on
previous year's twigs; scales greenish. Female flowers in
elongated clusters 1.2 to 1.9 cm long at the tips of new leafy
twigs; scales hairy, greenish.

**Simple, Not Lobed, Alternate**    97

**Fruit.** Small, ovoid, ribbed nut, 6 to 9 cm long, in the axil of a three-lobed, leaf-like bract about 25 mm long, borne in loose, hanging terminal clusters 10 to 15 cm long in midsummer. The brownish nut remains attached to the bract, which functions as a large wind-borne samara, and often remains on the tree long after the leaves have fallen.

**Distribution.** Throughout southern New England, Vermont except for Essex County, southern New Hampshire, and downeast Maine; in Canada, extreme southwestern Quebec and southeastern Ontario. Elsewhere throughout the eastern United States from New York (except the Adirondack Mountains) west to eastern Minnesota, south to east Texas, and to central Florida. Absent from the lower Mississippi River Valley and the Gulf Coast.

**Habitat.** American hornbeam generally occurs on deep, rich, moist soils or low, fertile, poorly drained sites along the edges of swamps and streams, commonly growing in association with red maple, black ash, yellow birch, and basswood. It is very shade-tolerant, common in the understory of moist deciduous forests.

**Notes:** Of the twenty-five species of trees in the genus *Carpinus,* only American hornbeam is found in North America. The wood is heavy, hard, tough, and strong, but of little commercial value because of its small size and poor form. The wood was used for tool handles. The seeds and nutlets are eaten primarily by ruffed grouse and gray squirrels in New England.

### In the Field
- Leaves very thin, smooth, finely toothed with (usually) unbranched veins
- Bark smooth, gray with fluted muscle-like ridges on the short crooked or leaning trunk
- Very slender twigs and small buds
- Small nuts in the axils of leaf-like three-lobed bracts, in long, hanging clusters
- Found in the open understory on rich, moist sites

# HOP HORNBEAM   Ostryer de Virginie

Ironwood
*Ostrya virginiana* (Mill.) K. Koch
Betulaceae: Birch Family

**Size and Form.** Hop hornbeam is a small
tree, up to 15 m tall and about 25 cm in
diameter, sometimes larger. The trunk is
normally very upright and straight, and
distinct to the top of the tree. The crown is
conical and wide-spreading with long
slender branches and twigs.

**Leaves.** Alternate, simple, 7 to 12 cm long, and 3 to 5 cm wide,
oblong, tapering to a sharp pointed tip, becoming progressively
larger toward the end of the shoot. The straight, parallel veins
each end in a sharp tooth, with several, somewhat smaller,
intervening teeth. Upper surface dark yellow-green, similar but

hairy beneath. Petiole short,
slender, and hairy, the hairs
usually gland-tipped. Autumn
color: clear yellow.

**Bark.** Gray-brown, thin, broken
into short, narrow, vertical strips
that are loose at both ends, giving
a scaly or shredded appearance.
On saplings, bark is smooth,
tight, chestnut brown.

**Twigs.** Slender, zigzag, narrower than the buds. Light brown at
first, becoming shiny reddish brown, and finally dull dark brown.

**Buds.** Oval, pointed, 4 to 6 mm long, green-brown to light
brown, divergent from the twig, bud scales longitudinally
striate, sparsely hairy, not in regular rows. True terminal bud
absent.

**Flowers.** April to May, with the leaves, monoecious. Male
flowers in drooping catkins 15 to 50 mm long, in twos or threes
at twig tips; in winter, visible but short, stiff, erect. Female

flowers in pairs, elongated clusters at the tips of new leafy shoots, each flower in a hairy sac-like bract.

**Fruit.** Small, flattened nut in September, 5 to 8 mm long, enclosed in an oval, grayish inflated sac-like bract, resembling hops, about 15 mm long, borne in clusters of four to ten, on slender, hairy stems.

**Distribution.** Hop hornbeam occurs throughout New England except for outer Cape Cod and Nantucket, and in adjacent Canada from Nova Scotia (except the southeast coast) through southern New Brunswick and southern Quebec. Elsewhere, throughout most of the eastern United States and adjacent Canada from New York (except the Adirondack Mountains) and southern Ontario west to southeastern Manitoba, south to east Texas, and east to northwestern Florida. Absent from the lower Mississippi River Valley, the Gulf Coast, and the coastal plain from New Jersey to Florida.

**Habitat.** Well-drained, often rocky slopes and ridges, never on poorly drained sites in New England. Very shade-tolerant, slow-growing, and relatively long-lived. Most common in the understories of broadleaf forests, especially oak-maple, oak-hickory, and beech-maple forests.

**Notes:** The word *Ostrya* is from the Greek *ostrua,* a tree with hard wood. One of the very few trees that always occupies a subdominant position—never a canopy tree. A handsome ornamental but difficult to transplant because of the deep taproot. Known as ironwood, the exceedingly tough wood was used for mallets, levers, sleigh runners, wagon tongues, wheel rims, and spokes, as well as other items in earlier times. The wildlife food value is limited but the buds and nuts are an important food of ruffed grouse in many areas.

### *In the Field*
- Leaves with fine hairs on upper surface, veins often branched
- Bark shredded, shaggy, on a straight trunk
- Small catkins in late summer to winter in threes and fours
- Fruits in hop-like clusters, each enclosed in a bladder-like sac

# HACKBERRY    Micocoulier occidental

American hackberry, common hackberry, sugarberry
*Celtis occidentalis* L.
Ulmaceae: Elm Family

**Size and Form.** Hackberry is normally a
medium-sized tree, 12 to 18 m tall and 30
to 60 cm in diameter. Open-grown trees
branch 3 to 4 m above the ground into
several large limbs with many slender,
horizontal, zigzag branches forming a
broad, irregular crown. Forest-grown trees
have a tall, straight trunk and a slender crown.

**Leaves.** Alternate, simple, variable
in size, generally 5 to 14 cm long,
and about half as wide; ovate or
ovate-lanceolate, apex long-
pointed and base asymmetrical,
margins coarsely serrate above the
base. Leaves thin, light green or
bluish green above, pale beneath,
with conspicuous veins that are
hairy beneath; lowest pair of veins
originate at an acute angle just
below the base of the blade; hairy.
Leaf surface is smooth or somewhat rough to the touch. Petiole
short, slender, and hairy. Autumn color: green until late
autumn, then turning light yellow.

**Bark.** Fairly thin, light gray to silvery or yellowish brown,
smooth on young stems, becoming irregularly ridged with
distinctive blocky, corky, wart-like projections that are stratified
in cross section.

**Twigs.** New twigs slender, greenish, covered with fine hairs,
becoming smooth and tinged with reddish brown in the first
winter; pith small, white, closely divided into small chambers
by transverse partitions; vein scars two or three.

**Buds.** Terminal bud absent, end and lateral buds light brown, 3 to 6 mm long, oval, sharp-pointed, flattened with 5 or more scales and the tip close to the twig.

**Flowers.** May, with or soon after the leaves, monoecious. Small, greenish yellow male flowers in small clusters at the base of the new shoot, female flowers usually single in the axils of the upper leaves.

**Fruit.** A berry-like drupe with a wrinkled stone, ripening in early autumn; solitary on a slender stalk, round, smooth, thin-fleshed, dark purple, 6 to 8 mm in diameter, edible, becoming deeply puckered, and persisting on the tree in winter.

**Distribution.** Hackberry is distributed widely in the eastern United States and southernmost Canada, occurring from southern New England and the Champlain lowlands west through central New York, southern Quebec and Ontario to North Dakota, south to Texas, Arkansas, Tennessee, and North Carolina. Range overlaps that of the closely related sugarberry (*Celtis laevigata*) in the south, with hackberry occurring on upland sites and sugarberry in the lowlands.

**Habitat.** Grows on a variety of soils and is moderately shade-tolerant. It is primarily a bottomland tree but it also occurs on alkaline upland soils. Hackberry occurs as a scattered tree in many types of forests; it rarely if ever occurs in pure stands.

**Notes:** The word *Celtis* is the classical Latin name of the African lotus, applied to hackberries because of the sweet fruit. Hackberry wood, though heavy, is soft and weak. Poor grades are sometimes used in crates and boxes; good grades in furniture. Hackberry is a very valuable wildlife tree, the fruits readily eaten by a wide variety of birds and mammals. Of particular value is the persistent nature of the fruits, hanging on the tree into the winter long after most other fruits are gone. A disease, "witches' broom," causes a rosette-like proliferation of the branch tips and is very characteristic.

### *In the Field*

- Leaf base asymmetrical, with three principal veins arising from the base
- Bark with corky warts
- Fruit dark purple, raisin-like when dried, covers a large seed
- Dense clusters of twigs, "witches' brooms," scattered throughout the crown

# AMERICAN ELM    Orme d'Amérique

White elm, water elm
*Ulmus americana* L.
Ulmaceae: Elm Family

**Size and Form.** The largest and most attractive of the North American elms, American elm is a large tree, 20 to 30 m tall and 50 to 120 cm in diameter. The trunk, buttressed at the base, normally divides 6 to 9 m above the ground into several large upright branches with drooping twigs to form a vase-shaped crown. Its graceful crown and deep shade made the American elm characteristic of city streets and towns throughout the eastern United States and adjacent Canada, but Dutch elm

disease has eliminated most of the large trees in many areas. Where mature individuals survive, they are among the largest trees in the East. The largest recorded specimen in Massachusetts is in Spencer; it has a circumference of 6.5 m (206 cm in diameter) and a height of 25 m. The crown spread is 29 m.

**Leaves.** Alternate, in two rows along the twig, simple, 10 to 15 cm long and about half as wide, oval with an asymmetrical base, doubly toothed; thick, firm, dark green and rough-textured above, pale and hairy beneath; fifteen to twenty veins per side, rarely forked (one or two on occasional leaf; petiole short and stout. Autumn color: dull yellow.

**Bark.** Thick, corky, gray or gray-brown, deeply fissured into broad, interlacing scaly ridges with age. In cross section, outer bark shows alternating whitish and brown layers.

**Twigs.** Slender, zigzag, initially greenish, turning gray-brown, normally hairless.

**Buds.** End and lateral buds brown, 3 to 6 cm long, oval, pointed, flattened, in two rows along the twig, oblique above the leaf scar, scales smooth or slightly hairy. True terminal bud absent.

**Flowers.** Early spring, before the leaves, small, mostly perfect, brown or brownish red, on slender stalks in loose clusters of eight to twenty.

**Fruit.** Samara, oval, 8 to 10 mm long and fringed with hairs, wing notched at tip, seed case distinct and centered in the wing, on long stalks. The fruits are produced in profusion, and ripen before the leaves are fully grown and fall soon after.

**Distribution.** American elm occurs throughout New England and adjacent Canada. It is found throughout eastern North America, ranging from Cape Breton Island in Nova Scotia west to central Ontario and southeastern Saskatchewan, south to northeastern Wyoming, central Texas, and central Florida, and north along the entire east coast.

**Habitat.** American elm is most common on flats and bottomlands throughout its range but is not restricted to these sites. Associated trees include black ash, red maple, silver maple, black birch, paper birch, gray birch, and black spruce. It readily colonizes disturbed sites, but best growth occurs on rich, well-drained sandy or gravelly loams.

**Notes:** *Ulmus* is the classical name of the elms, from the Saxon word *ulm*. Once a common tree of pastures and roadsides, American elm—also the state tree of Massachusetts—has been almost eliminated as a large tree by Dutch elm disease and phloem necrosis. Young trees fruit prolifically, and aggressively colonize open disturbed sites, so the tree is not in danger of extinction. The wood is heavy, hard, strong, and tough, and was once used in wagon wheel hubs and for wooden-spoked automobile wheels. Interlocking grain makes it difficult to split; it is used in furniture, crates, barrels, bowls, and veneer. Baltimore orioles commonly nest in the drooping twigs of mature elms. Flower buds, flowers, and fruit are eaten by gray squirrels. The seeds are eaten by small mammals and birds.

### In the Field

- Leaf margins have large and small teeth, veins simple, rarely forked
- Bark cross section shows alternating light and dark layers
- Samaras are oval; the wing is deeply notched and the edge hairy
- Trunk distinctly buttressed at the base
- Mature trees have a distinct vase shape with drooping branch tips

# SLIPPERY ELM    Orme rouge

Red elm, gray elm
*Ulmus rubra* Muhl.
Ulmaceae: Elm Family

**Size and Form.** Slippery elm is a medium-
sized tree, 15 to 21 m tall and 30 to 60 cm in
diameter, and has a trunk that is both
longer and more limb-free than that of the
larger American elm. Also, the branches of
slippery elm are spreading and ascending,
forming a broad, irregular spreading
crown, unlike the drooping branches of American elm's vase-
shaped crown.

**Leaves.** Alternate, simple, 10 to 20
cm long and about half as wide,
oval to elliptical, widest above the
middle, with an asymmetrical
base, doubly toothed, thick, firm,
dark green and very rough-
textured above, paler and hairy
beneath; two or more lateral veins
fork near the margin (generally
more than in American elm);
fragrant; petiole short, stout, hairy.
Autumn color: yellow brown.

**Bark.** Thick, dark red-brown, with shallow fissures and large,
loose plates, more parallel than that of American elm. The
outer bark layers are solid brown in cross section, not layered
as in American elm. The common name, slippery elm, refers
to the inner bark, which is mucilaginous and somewhat
aromatic.

**Twigs.** Moderately stout, bright green and hairy when new,
becoming brown or grayish; leaf scars covered with a corky
layer, pores prominent.

**Buds.** End and lateral buds in two rows along the twig; blunt,
dark brown or black, scales covered with reddish-colored hairs,

4 to 6 mm long; flower buds large, round, with orange hairs at the tips. True terminal bud absent.

**Flowers.** March or April, before the leaves, mostly perfect, on short stalks in three-flowered clusters.

**Fruit.** Samara, appearing in May, almost circular, one-seeded, short-stalked in dense clusters, the seed cover brown and hairy, wings smooth, 1.8 to 2 cm long, with a shallow notch at the tip.

**Distribution.** Slippery elm is uncommon in Maine, New Hampshire, and most of adjacent Canada. It occurs from Vermont (except the Northeast Kingdom) south through central and western Massachusetts, Connecticut, and Rhode Island, west to New York, extreme southern Quebec and Ontario, to southeastern North Dakota, south to central Texas, east to northwestern Florida and Georgia. It is most abundant in the Lake states and the Midwest.

**Habitat.** Best growth occurs on moist, rich soils of floodplains, along streams and adjacent slopes. Also grows on dry hillsides with limestone soils. Associated tree species are many because slippery elm grows in mixtures with other hardwoods on a wide variety of sites.

**Notes:** The word *rubra* is Latin for "red." The wood is hard and strong, similar to American elm, but considered inferior to that species. It is not an important lumber tree and when cut is sold as soft elm along with American elm. The tree is susceptible to Dutch elm disease. The fall-ripening seeds are consumed by wood duck, gray and red squirrels, and birds including purple finches and rose-breasted grosbeaks, among others.

> **In the Field**
> - Leaves large, very rough-textured, widest above the middle, generally two or more forked veins
> - Buds blunt, hairy, dark purple-brown
> - Inner bark of twigs slimy
> - Bark layers uniformly brown in cross section
> - The samara has a hairy seed case and a nearly circular, smooth wing

# AMERICAN CHESTNUT   Châtaignier d'Amérique

Chinkapin
*Castanea dentata* (Marsh.) Borkh.
Fagaceae: Beech Family

**Size and Form.** Before the arrival of the chestnut blight early in the twentieth century, American chestnut was a large, magnificent tree, up to 35 m tall and 100 cm or more in diameter. Now it seldom reaches 10 m tall and occurs as a doomed understory tree, commonly arising from root collar sprouts, although some trees do produce seed. Such seed does not produce blight-resistant trees.

**Leaves.** Alternate, simple, 15 to 28 cm long, 5 to 7 cm wide, widest in the middle and tapering at both ends, coarsely toothed with the tips of the teeth slightly incurved, veins extending beyond the tip of each tooth to form a short, curved bristle; leaves are thin and smooth, a dull light green or yellow-green above, lighter beneath; stems short, stout, faintly pubescent. Autumn color: yellow-brown.

**Bark.** Thin, smooth, and dark brown on young trees, separating into shallow fissures and wide, flat ridges. Usually only the beginning stages of bark separation are seen before the young tree dies.

**Twigs.** Stout, shiny, yellow-green when new, becoming olive-green and then brown or red-brown, with numerous light-colored pores. The pith resembles a five-pointed star in cross section. Leaf scars long-oval or rounded-triangular and somewhat raised, with numerous vein scars.

**Buds.** Terminal bud absent. Lateral buds 6 mm long, egg-shaped, pointed, divergent, dark chestnut brown, with two or three hairless scales.

**Flowers.** June or July, after the leaves, monoecious. Male catkins slender, 15 to 20 cm long, stiff, found on short stalks near the base of new shoots. Female flowers solitary or in clusters of two to three at the base of some male catkins.

**Fruit.** A nut in small clusters of one to three enclosed in a round, bristly husk or bur with branched spines, 5 to 6 cm in diameter, which splits into four parts, exposing the velvety inner surface. Nuts 1.5 to 2.5 cm wide, flattened on one side, dull chestnut brown with whitish down near the tip, sweet and edible.

**Distribution.** In New England, American chestnut occurs primarily in Massachusetts, Connecticut, Rhode Island, and southeastern New Hampshire. Also west to Minnesota, south to Mississippi and Florida. In Canada, it was once a prominent tree in southern Ontario, but is now rare.

**Habitat.** American chestnut grows on a variety of sites but grows best on well-drained sands and gravels, usually mixed with other broad-leaved trees, especially oaks. It reproduces vegetatively from stump sprouts, which perpetuates its presence, but precludes the development of resistance to the chestnut blight disease.

**Notes:** *Castanea* is the classical name of the chestnut tree; the word *dentata* means "toothed," referring to the leaf margins. American chestnut was once a very valuable tree, for both its hard, strong, decay-resistant wood and for its nuts. A century ago, the nuts were a valuable and abundant wildlife food, readily eaten by deer, bears, and many birds and mammals. The chestnut blight (*Endothia parasitica*), common in Europe for a long time, probably entered North America on stock imported from Asia in 1904. The effect on oak-chestnut forests was immediate and devastating, and a valuable wood and wildlife resource was lost. Scattered mature trees survive in parts of chestnut's former range, including several mature trees in Maine. The American Chestnut Foundation established a backcross-breeding program with the blight-resistant Chinese chestnut in 1989 to produce an American chestnut tree that retains no Chinese characteristics other than blight resistance. Currently, the most advanced trees have at least 94 percent American genes. Seeds for trees having the characteristics necessary for restoration are expected to be available in the near future (http://www.acf.org/).

> ### In the Field
> - Leaves alternate, long and narrow with straight, parallel veins, each ending in a prominent tooth with a bristle tip
> - Buds and twigs smooth
> - Fruit a cluster of burs, each of which split into four parts to reveal the nut
> - Twig in cross section reveals a star-shaped pith

# AMERICAN BEECH    Hêtre á grandes feuilles

Beech
*Fagus grandifolia* Ehrh.
Fagaceae: Beech Family

**Size and Form.** American beech is a medium-sized to large tree, 18 to 26 m tall and 50 to 100 cm in diameter. In the forest, it is tall and slender, the trunk often branch-free for a considerable height with short branches and a narrow crown. Open-grown trees have a short, thick trunk and numerous slender spreading branches forming a broad, rounded crown. The shallow, extensive root system commonly produces root suckers in abundance.

**Leaves.** Alternate, simple, blades 7 to 12 cm long and about half as wide, oblong, pointed at the tip, wedge-shaped or rounded at the base, coarsely toothed; veins parallel, a vein ending in each tooth; leaves thin, smooth, leathery, dark bluish green to green above, light yellow-green beneath; petiole short, stout, and hairy. Dried leaves persist over winter on young trees, and sometimes on the lower branches of open-grown mature trees. Autumn color: dark yellow-brown.

**Bark.** The thin, smooth, light blue-gray or ash-gray bark is probably the most characteristic feature of American beech; often mottled with dark spots, and trees in parks and other public places are frequently disfigured by carved initials. In the forest, claw marks are commonly seen, made by black bears seeking beech nuts.

**Twigs.** Slender, shiny, zigzag, olive green turning brown, then gray.

**Buds.** Terminal and lateral buds cigar-shaped, slender, sharp-pointed; lateral buds offset above a leaf scar and angled widely from the twig, 15 to 25 mm long, brownish, with many bud scales, each with a gray, hairy margin. The buds near the twig end are larger than those farther back on the twig.

**Flowers.** April or May, with the leaves, monoecious. Male flowers in round clusters at the ends of pendulous stalks near the base of new leafy shoots. Female flowers are in small clusters of two to four in axils of leaves near the shoot tip, and appear as the leaves unfold.

**Fruit.** A nut, usually two, sometimes three, in a bristly red-brown husk or bur, borne on a stout hairy stalk; the husk opens in four parts, and persists on the shoot well after the nuts have fallen. The nut itself is 1 to 2 cm long, is three-sided and sharp-pointed, resembling a pyramid, reddish brown, sweet and edible. Good seed crops occur every three to five years.

**Distribution.** American beech occurs throughout New England and adjacent Canada. It is widely distributed throughout the eastern United States.

**Habitat.** American beech occurs on moist, well-drained slopes and rich bottomlands, as well as on dry-mesic sites in the northern part of its range. It generally does not occur on limestone soils except on the western edge of its range. American beech in New England and Canada commonly occurs with sugar maple, yellow birch, and eastern hemlock. It is slow-growing and very shade-tolerant; young trees may persist in the understory for many years.

**Notes:** The word *Fagus* is the Latin name of the beeches, from the Greek *fagein* (to eat) referring to the nuts; *grandifolia* means "large-leaved." American beech is highly susceptible to beech bark disease. The beech scale insect, *Cryptococcus fagisuga,* with the fungus *Nectria coccinea* var. *faginata* cause disfiguring cankers on the bark and may kill the tree. The wood, which is hard, tough, and close-grained, is strong but not durable in contact with the ground. Uses include flooring, furniture, turned products and novelties, veneer, plywood, pulpwood, fuelwood, clothes pins, and woodenware. The nuts or mast are a highly attractive food for wildlife, including chipmunks and squirrels, black bears, white-tailed deer, foxes, wild turkeys, ruffed grouse, ducks, most woodpeckers, and bluejays.

### In the Field
- Bark smooth and gray regardless of age
- Leaves with nine to fourteen straight, parallel veins per side, each ending in a tooth
- Buds long, slender with many scales, sharp-pointed
- Fruit a three-sided nut in a four-parted bristly husk or bur
- The commonly planted European beech, *Fagus sylvatica* L., has finely pubescent gray buds and fruit, and rounder, more finely toothed leaves

# CHESTNUT OAK     Chêne châtaignier

Rock chestnut oak, tan bark oak, rock oak
*Quercus prinus* L. [*Q. montana* Willd.]
Fagaceae: Beech Family

**Size and Form.** Chestnut oak is generally
a small to medium-sized tree, 7.5 to 15 m
tall with a relatively long trunk topped by
a series of stout spreading branches
forming a broad, open rounded crown.

**Leaves.** Long-oval, 12.5 to 23 cm long, about half as wide, and
widest near the middle (often slightly above or below the

middle); the margin is crenate or
round-toothed; leaves thick,
yellow-green above, paler and
somewhat hairy beneath.
Autumn color: russet.

**Bark.** Dark brown to almost
black, firm, with deep fissures
and vertical ridges. Not scaly.

**Twigs.** Stout, smooth, light
reddish brown.

**Buds.** Egg-shaped, the lateral buds at the tip of the twig
clustered around the large terminal bud; buds light brown and
hairy, 6 to 12.5 mm long. Lateral buds along the twig diverge
widely from the twig.

**Flowers.** May, when leaves are about a quarter grown,
monoecious. Male flowers borne on long hanging catkins 5 to
7.5 cm long, produced from either the lateral buds or from
between the scales of the terminal bud. Seed flowers borne
singly or in clusters of two or three on short stalks in the leaf
axils on new shoots.

**Fruit.** Acorns borne singly or in pairs (rarely three) on a short
stalk, maturing at the end of the first summer. Egg-shaped light
brown, smooth and shiny, 19 to 15 mm long, a third to half of

its length enclosed by the cup. The rim of the cup has no fringe. Good seed crops are infrequent.

**Distribution.** Chestnut oak extends from extreme southwestern Maine west through southern New Hampshire and the Champlain Lowlands of Vermont and New York to extreme southern Ontario and southeastern Michigan, south through southern New England to Georgia, and generally west of the Coastal Plain to northeastern Mississippi. In Massachusetts, it is most common from Worcester County eastward, but also occurs in the Blue Hills south of Boston. It is endangered in Maine.

**Habitat.** Chestnut oak is a tree of dry upland sites—sandy, gravelly, or rocky soils of ridge tops and upper slopes. The best growth occurs in the mountains of the western Carolinas and Tennessee.

**Notes:** *Quercus* is the classical Latin name of the oaks, said to be derived from Celtic for "fine tree"; *prinus* is the classical name for European oak. The wood is similar to that of white oak and used for similar purposes (see white oak, page 135). The sweet acorns of chestnut oak are consumed readily by many wildlife species including deer, bears, turkeys, and squirrels. Long-lived and slow-growing, chestnut oak can reach 400 years old.

> ### In the Field
> - Leaf margins with rounded teeth, a vein ending in each tooth (American chestnut has sharp-pointed teeth)
> - Bark thickly ridged and furrowed, not scaly
> - Acorn smooth, shiny, enclosed for a third to a half of its length by the thin, deep cap
> - Acorn cap rim not fringed

# YELLOW OAK  Chêne jaune

Yellow chestnut oak, rock oak, chinquapin oak, chinkapin oak
*Quercus muehlenbergii* Engelm.
Fagaceae: Beech Family

**Size and Form.** Yellow oak, formerly
known as chinquapin oak or chinkapin
oak, is a medium-sized tree, 18 to 24 m tall
and 30 to 60 cm in diameter. It has a
straight, tapering trunk, often buttressed
at the base, that extends well into the
crown. Erect, short branches form a
narrow, round-topped crown.

**Leaves.** Alternate, simple, with
blades 5 to 15 cm long, 4 to 8 cm
wide, pointed at both ends,
somewhat lance-shaped or
oblong-oval, with coarse, sharp-
pointed teeth, eight to fourteen
teeth per side; leaves thick, firm,
and shiny, yellowish green above,
light green and hairy beneath,
petiole slender, 1 to 3.5 cm long.
Autumn color: russet.

**Bark.** Thin, silvery gray or ashy white, rough and flaky with
shallow fissures.

**Twigs.** Slender with light-colored pores, smooth, greenish
when new, becoming brownish gray.

**Buds.** Terminal bud about 4 to 6 mm long, conical, pointed,
with thin chestnut-brown scales.

**Flowers.** May to June, with the leaves, monoecious. Male catkin
hairy, about 7 to 10 cm long, with yellow flowers. Female
flowers stalkless or on short spikes, very hairy or wooly.

**Fruit.** Acorns, ripening in autumn of first season; stalkless or
short-stalked; cup deep with thin, small, hairy scales, enclosing

a third to half of the nut. Nut oval, 1.3 to 2.5 cm long, dark brown to blackish, white-downy at the tip, kernel fairly sweet.

**Distribution.** Yellow oak is found in disjunct populations in the Champlain Valley in Vermont and the southwestern corner of Massachusetts and northwestern corner and Housatonic River Valley in Connecticut. Range extends west to southern Ontario, and southeastern Minnesota, south to central Texas and Florida. Yellow oak is uncommon or rare over most of its range.

**Habitat.** Yellow oak grows on limestone soils and well-drained upland slopes, usually with other hardwoods. Yellow oak is rarely the predominant tree, growing as an associate with white oak, northern red oak, sugar maple, red maple, and white ash where it occurs in New England and Canada. Elsewhere in its range, it also grows on sand dunes.

**Notes:** For the meaning of *Quercus* see chestnut oak, page 116; *muehlenbergii* is after Gotthilf Heinrich Ernest Muhlenberg (1753–1815), an American botanist. The wood is similar to that of white oak and used for similar purposes (see white oak, page 135). Commercially unimportant because of its small size and lack of abundance, but the acorns are a valuable wildlife food.

> ### In the Field
> - Leaves dark green, shiny above, elliptical to lanceolate, with eight to fourteen sharp-pointed teeth, somewhat similar to those of American chestnut
> - Bark ridges flaky, light gray to ashy-white
> - Trunk tapering from buttressed butt and extending well into the crown
> - Acorns similar to white oak but smaller and with densely hairy scales; cap enclosing a third to a half of the nut

# SWAMP WHITE OAK    Chêne bicolore

Swamp oak
*Quercus bicolor* Willd.
Fagaceae: Beech Family

**Size and Form.** Swamp white oak, in
contrast to white oak, is a small to
medium-sized tree with a more or less
ragged crown. Swamp white oak is
generally 15 to 21 m tall and 60 or more cm
in diameter, with an open crown of
ascending upper branches and drooping
lower branches and rather bushy leaf clusters.

**Leaves.** Alternate, simple, blades
12 to 18 cm long and 7 to 12 cm
wide, oval to oblong, widest above
the middle with a wedge-shaped
base; coarsely wavy-toothed,
rarely lobed; thick, firm, a shiny
dark green above, whitish and
finely hairy beneath, sharp
contrast in color between top and
bottom surfaces. Petiole stout,
about 1 cm long. Autumn color:
yellow-brown or orange.

**Bark.** Thick, gray-brown, deeply fissured with long, flat-
topped, scaly ridges with age.

**Twigs.** Stout with light-colored pores, new shoots shiny green,
turning red-brown or dark brown with a whitish bloom.

**Buds.** Terminal bud 3 to 6 mm long, round or blunt-oval, light
brown, usually hairless but sometimes with soft hairs on the
upper half. Small, round lateral buds diverge from twig
clustered toward tip of twig.

**Flowers.** May to June, with the leaves, monoecious. Male
flowers in hairy catkins 7 to 10 cm long; female flowers very
hairy in few-flowered spikes, on long hairy stalks.

**Fruit.** Acorn, maturing in autumn of first season, usually in pairs (sometimes singly) on downy stalks 3 to 8 cm long, cup is bowl-shaped with swollen loose scales, rim usually slightly fringed and enclosing a third of the nut. Nut 19 to 32 mm long, oval, light brown, with downy hairs at the tip, kernel white, somewhat sweet.

**Distribution.** Swamp white oak occurs primarily from southeastern New Hampshire through central and eastern Massachusetts south to southwestern Connecticut, up the Hudson River Valley, west through Pennsylvania and central Michigan to central Wisconsin, south to central Missouri and east to Ohio and New Jersey excluding the Coastal Plain. The range includes disjunct populations in southwestern Maine, the Champlain lowlands of Vermont and New York, southern Quebec, and scattered locations south of the contiguous range.

**Habitat.** Characteristic of low, wet, poorly drained soils, swamp borders, and river bottoms, where it is found with silver maple, red maple, eastern cottonwood, sycamore, red ash, black gum, American elm, and basswood. Not usually found where the water table is continuously high.

**Notes:** For the meaning of *Quercus,* see chestnut oak, page 116; *bicolor* means "two-colored," from the Latin *bis* (two) and *color,* referring to the leaves. Rapid-growing, fairly long-lived (300 to 350 years). The wood is similar to that of white oak and used for similar purposes (see white oak, page 135). The acorns are an important source of hard mast for a number of wildlife species, and make up a large part of the diet of wood ducks and other waterfowl.

> ### In the Field
> - Leaves shiny dark green above, very pale and finely hairy beneath, variable in shape
> - Wavy-toothed, rarely lobed, and widest above the middle
> - Acorns on long stalks
> - Lower branches drooping
> - Found on moist sites

## Group 8
### Simple, Not Lobed, Opposite

# FLOWERING DOGWOOD    Cornouiller fleuri

Dogwood, white dogwood, cornel
*Cornus florida* L.
Cornaceae: Dogwood Family

**Size and Form.** Flowering dogwood is
a small tree, rarely more than 10 m tall,
with a short, crooked trunk 15 to 30 cm
in diameter. Flowering dogwood is a
popular ornamental tree; attractive in
all seasons. It is slow-growing with a
flat-topped crown and whorls of wide-

spreading branches. The showy petal-like bracts are not petals
but make the inflorescences appear to be single large flowers.
Epicormic branching commonly occurs on the trunk.

**Leaves.** Opposite, simple,
clustered at the ends of the twigs,
7 to 12 cm long, 5 to 8 cm wide;
broad-oval to elliptical, margin
entire, thick, dark green above
and pale and somewhat hairy
beneath with prominent veins
arching from the mid-rib
becoming parallel to the margins.
Autumn colors: rose to scarlet and
violet.

**Bark.** Thin, reddish brown to gray or black, checked into
rectangular plates or plate-like scales.

**Twigs.** Slender, pale green with whitish hairs, becoming red or
yellow-green the first winter, later becoming light brown or
purple-gray, and hairless. Pith white or tan, continuous.

**Buds.** Terminal bud narrow-conical, pointed, greenish to reddish, downy, with one pair of bud scales that meet at the edges but do not overlap against the twig; lateral buds minute, pressed against the twig; the terminal pair of leaf scars raised, connected on each side by a U- or V-shaped line; flower buds gray, stalked, and spherical or pagoda-shaped.

**Flowers.** May or June; when the leaves are about half-grown the true flowers are small and tubular, perfect, yellow-green, in dense clusters surrounded by (normally) four large showy, white petal-like bracts forming a "flower" up to 6 cm across, borne on short, stout, stalks.

**Fruit.** An oval, scarlet drupe, 13 mm long and 6 mm in diameter, containing a two-celled bony stone usually with two seeds; ripens from September to October; in clusters of three to six.

**Distribution.** Southwestern Maine, southern New Hampshire, Vermont, and throughout southern New England, south to northern Florida, west to Michigan and east Texas. Endangered in Maine.

**Habitat.** Typically an old-field or forest understory tree; wide site tolerances but usually found on rich, moist, well-drained soils, most commonly at forest edges in New England, but also on south or west-facing slopes. Intolerant of frequently flooded or extremely dry sites, especially upper slopes or ridges. In New England, it commonly is associated with white and red oaks, sassafras, black cherry, red maple, and white pine.

**Notes:** The name *Cornus* is derived from the Latin word for "horn," referring to the hardness of the wood, and *florida* from the Latin *floris,* meaning "blossom." The common name, dogwood, refers to former use of the bark to treat dogs' mange. The wood is heavy, hard, strong, tough, and close-grained, taking a smooth finish, and resistant to abrasion. It once was used primarily to make shuttles and bobbins for weaving, but also was used for turned items such as spools and pulleys. Flowering dogwood is a valuable food source for birds and other wildlife. More than thirty-five bird species, especially thrushes, catbirds, mockingbirds, and most woodpeckers feed on the fruits as do several mammals such as chipmunks, gray squirrels, rabbits, foxes, and deer. Seed dispersal is primarily by birds and mammals. A number of horticultural varieties have been developed with pendulous branches, red or pink bracts, or yellow fruits. It is a widely planted ornamental, although dogwood anthracnose disease is a problem in the Northeast. In New England, wild specimens normally are resistant, but planted trees commonly show signs of disease—typically profuse epicormic branching—in ten to fifteen years. Flowering dogwood has very rapidly decomposing leaves, three to four times faster than hickories and ten times faster than oaks; the leaves are considered a soil improver because they are especially rich in calcium.

### In the Field
- Leaves opposite, margins entire, veins arch upward parallel to the margins
- Terminal pair of leaf scars raised, connected on each side by a U- or V-shaped line
- Bark very blocky with distinct furrows
- Flower buds gray, button or pagoda-shaped
- Inflorescence with four showy white bracts
- Fruits bright scarlet drupes in clusters

# Group 9
## Simple, Lobed, Alternate

## SASSAFRAS    Sassafras officinal

White sassafras
*Sassafras albidum* (Nutt.) Nees
Lauraceae: Laurel Family

**Size and Form.** Sassafras is a small tree, up to 15 m tall, 20 to 60 cm in diameter. The trunk is short and stout and often contorted. Short, stout branches spread at right angles to form a flat-topped crown. In the northern part of its range on poor sites, sassafras is short and shrubby.

**Leaves.** Deciduous, alternate, simple, 8 to 15 cm long, 5 to 10 cm wide. Usually leaves of three different shapes are found on the same tree: somewhat elliptical, two-lobed (mitten-shaped), and three-lobed. Lobes are finger-like with broad, rounded sinuses; margin entire, dull dark green above, paler below, which may be smooth or covered with short, soft hairs. The leaves have a spicy odor when bruised. Autumn color: bright red, yellow, and orange.

**Bark.** Thick, dark reddish brown, aromatic, with deep furrows and flat-topped ridges crossed by horizontal cracks.

**Twigs.** Stout, smooth and shiny or slightly hairy, brittle, green, turning reddish brown, aromatic. The pith is large and white. Shoots may branch freely the first season.

**Buds.** Terminal bud is 8 to 15 mm long, ovoid, pointed, green, flower bearing. Lateral buds are much smaller and divergent.

**Flowers.** May, with emerging leaves, dioecious. The greenish yellow flowers develop in loose, drooping, few-flowered clusters.

**Fruit.** A berry-like, oval, fleshy fruit, 8 to 13 mm long, shiny, dark blue, containing a single seed within a hard covering; falling soon after maturity in September or October The fruit is borne in a shallow cup on a long, thick, bright red stalk that persists after the fruit falls.

**Distribution.** Common in southern New England, restricted to southern areas in Maine, New Hampshire, and Vermont. Rare in Canada; occurs in southern Ontario north of Lake Erie from the western end of Lake Ontario west to southernmost Lake Huron.

**Habitat.** Sassafras can be found on all types of soils within its range. It grows best along forest edges or in open woods on moist, well-drained, sandy loams. Also found on disturbed sites, along fencerows, and in old fields where it forms small clones from root sprouts. Associates include oaks, white ash, aspens, red maple, sugar maple, American beech, eastern redcedar, hickories, American hornbeam, and hop hornbeam.

**Notes:** Sassafras is not an important commercial timber species, especially in the northern part of its range. The heartwood is gray or grayish brown with a spicy odor and taste. It is very resistant to decay, making it good for fence posts. Oil of sassafras is distilled from the bark of the trunks and roots. It is used to flavor medicines, candy, root beer, tobacco, and to perfume some soaps. Great crested flycatchers, kingbirds, and phoebes, normally insect-eaters, consume sassafras fruits, as do mockingbirds, most thrushes, and towhees, among others.

### *In the Field*
- Leaves of three different shapes are found on the same tree: somewhat elliptical, two-lobed (mitten-shaped), and three-lobed
- Spicy aroma in leaves, buds, twigs, bark, roots, and wood
- Shiny, dark blue, fleshy fruit on a thick, bright red stalk
- Large, white pith

# YELLOW-POPLAR  Tulipier de Virginie

Tulip tree, tulip poplar, white-poplar, whitewood
*Liriodendron tulipifera* L.
Magnoliaceae: Magnolia Family

**Size and Form.** Yellow-poplar is a large tree up to 35 m tall and 60 to 90 cm in diameter, even larger where it grows best on deep, rich, well-drained soils on coves and lower slopes in the southern Appalachian Mountains. In the forest, the trunk is tall, straight, and branch-free to a small, oblong, rather open crown. In the open, the crown forms a narrow pyramid or is oblong with branches extending almost to the ground.

**Leaves.** Deciduous, alternate, and simple; 10 to 15 cm in diameter, mostly four-lobed (sometimes six-lobed); base and tip appearing cut off, tip broadly notched, margin entire. Leaves are dark green, smooth, and shiny above, dull green and paler below. Petioles are slender and long. Autumn color: yellow.

**Bark.** On young trees green and smooth with small white spots; becoming thick, brownish, and deeply furrowed with rounded, interlacing ridges and grayish crevices. The inner bark is bitter and aromatic.

**Twigs.** Stout, smooth, shiny, reddish brown, becoming dark gray. The pith is solid, banded at intervals.

**Buds.** Terminal buds 13 to 25 mm long, flattened, "duck-billed" in appearance, with two outer scales, dark red covered with a white bloom. Lateral buds are similar but much smaller, 3 to 13 mm long, divergent. Stipule scars encircle the twig.

**Flowers.** May to June, after the leaves appear. Yellow-poplar flowers are large, 4 to 5 cm wide, showy, solitary, perfect, with six greenish yellow petals, resembling a tulip in shape.

**Fruit.** Winged, 3 to 5 cm long in an erect, cone-like aggregate of winged seeds 4 to 8 cm long, light brown in color; the slender, pointed axis often persists after the seeds have separated. The wing is long and flat, with a small angled seed case at the base bearing one or two seeds.

**Distribution.** Found throughout Connecticut, most of Rhode Island, and adjacent southern Massachusetts, and sporadically in western Vermont. It is widespread to the south and west in the United States. In Canada, occurs in southern Ontario in a narrow band along the north shore of Lake Erie, along the south shore of Lake Huron, and on the Niagara Peninsula.

**Habitat.** Found on deep, moist, well-drained soils; on bottomland, along streams, and on moist mountain slopes. Associates include white, black, and northern red oak, ash, beech, sugar maple, black gum, flowering dogwood, and hickories.

**Notes:** Yellow-poplar is one of the tallest hardwoods in the Eastern United States and a valuable timber species. The wood is straight grained, uniform in texture, and moderate to light in weight. The sapwood is creamy-white, from which the common names white-poplar and whitewood derive. The heartwood is green or yellow to tan with greenish cast. Uses include lumber, veneer, pulpwood, furniture, especially interior furniture parts, dimension stock, musical instruments, sporting goods, pallets, and particleboard. Because of its shiny green leaves, showy flowers, and exceptional form, it is a widely planted ornamental in places that can accommodate its large size. It has value as a honey tree. It is not of exceptional importance as a wildlife tree but its seeds are eaten by a number of birds and small mammals.

***In the Field***

- Trunk tall and straight, branch-free to a small, oblong, rather open crown
- Leaves dark green, mostly four-lobed, base and tip appearing cut off, tip broadly notched, margin smooth
- Terminal buds flattened, "duck-billed" in appearance, with two dark red outer scales
- Large, showy, greenish yellow, tulip-shaped flowers
- Fruit in an erect, light brown, cone-like aggregate of winged seeds, on a persistent slender axis

# WHITE MULBERRY    Mûrier blanc

*Morus alba* L.
Moraceae: Mulberry Family

**Size and Form.** White mulberry is a short-lived, small, spreading tree up to 12 m tall, native to eastern Asia. The short,

thick trunk is 20 to 40 cm in diameter, separating into several stout limbs, spreading into a broad, bushy crown with a profusion of fine twigs.

**Leaves.** Alternate, simple, 5 to 10 cm long, almost as wide, generally oval, variably lobed or unlobed. The leaf shape varies with the tree's stage of development: young trees (and sprouts from old trees) have a high proportion of many-lobed leaves; mature trees tend to have unlobed leaves; margins toothed with big triangular teeth, thin, shiny, light green above, paler beneath; the smooth petiole exudes a milky sap when cut. Autumn color: yellow.

**Bark.** Fairly thick, light to dark gray, becoming orange-brown with shallow furrows and flat ridges, the orange inner layers visible in the fissures.

**Twigs.** Slender, zigzag, somewhat swollen at the leaf scars, new growth red-brown and hairy, becoming smooth and yellow-brown or orange-brown. Twigs exude a milky sap when cut.

**Buds.** End and lateral buds oval to somewhat pyramidal, 3 to 4 mm long, shiny, tan-orange, tight against the twig, offset to above the leaf scar, bud scales uniform in color. Terminal bud absent.

**Flowers.** May or June, with the leaves, dioecious. Male flowers in dense catkins, 1 to 3 cm long on short stalks; female flowers also in dense catkins on short stalks.

**Fruit.** Clusters of drupes in June to July, 1 to 2 cm long, white or pinkish, sweet, edible, blackberry-like in form.

**Distribution.** Native to China, long cultivated in Europe and North America. White mulberry is widely naturalized in cities in the eastern United States and eastern Canada.

**Habitat.** Nearly any upland soil or habitat, waste places, fencerows, forest edges, city lots. Thrives in harsh urban conditions, but generally does not invade forests, as it is shade-intolerant.

**Notes:** *Alba* is Latin for "white," referring to the white fruit. White mulberry is a fast-growing tree that was introduced to eastern North America in colonial times in an effort to create a silk industry. The leaves are the food of the silkworm. The roots spread vigorously and readily clog drain pipes. Although the fruits are highly attractive to birds and mammals, which disseminate the seed, white mulberry is not recommended as an ornamental because it is an invasive exotic. A sterile cultivar with drooping branches was developed for such use and is sometimes seen in parks and estates.

> ### In the Field
> - Leaves shiny green, variously lobed or unlobed; young trees or sprouts have more lobed leaves than do mature trees
> - Broken stem or cut bark exudes milky sap
> - Bark shows orange inner bark in the fissures between ridges
> - Fruit white or pinkish, shaped like a blackberry
> - Usually in waste places or urban habitats, not in natural forest habitats

# RED MULBERRY   Mûrier rouge

*Morus rubra* L.
Moraceae: Mulberry Family

**Size and Form.** Red mulberry is a small tree, up to 15 m tall and 25 to 35 cm in diameter. The trunk is short, soon separating into thick spreading branches forming a dense, rounded crown with slender twigs.

**Leaves.** Alternate, simple, ovate, lobed and unlobed leaves occurring on the same tree (although lobed leaves are more abundant on young trees); blades 8 to 24 cm long, nearly as wide, base heart-shaped, somewhat asymmetrical, coarsely toothed; thin, dark blue-green or yellow-green and smooth or rough above, pale and somewhat downy beneath; petiole 2 to 5 cm long, smooth, exuding a milky juice when cut. Autumn color: yellow.

**Bark.** Reddish brown or dark brown with a red or yellow tinge, thin, scaly, separating into long flaky plates.

**Twigs.** Slender, somewhat zigzag, green and somewhat downy, becoming smooth and light or orange-brown; exuding a milky juice when cut.

**Buds.** Lateral and end buds broadly oval, asymmetrical, pointed, 5 to 8 mm long, light brown and shiny, angling out from the twig and offset to one side above the leaf scar, six to eight bud scales with brown margins, arranged in two rows. Terminal bud absent. Leaf scars raised, with five or more vein scars.

**Flowers.** May or June, with the leaves; usually dioecious, sometimes monoecious. Male flowers in dense catkins 2 to 5 cm

**Simple, Lobed, Alternate**   133

long in leaf axils; female flowers in dense catkins, on short, hairy stalks in the leaf axils.

**Fruit.** Clusters of drupes, in July to August, blackberry-like, about 2.5 to 3 cm long, initially bright red, turning dark purple. Sweet, juicy, edible.

**Distribution.** Red mulberry is uncommon in New England and rare in Canada, where small populations exist in extreme southern Ontario. It is widespread elsewhere in the eastern United States, from extreme southeastern New York and southernmost Ontario to southeastern Minnesota, south to central Texas, and east to southern Florida. Endangered in Massachusetts and Connecticut.

**Habitat.** Deep, moist soils, forested floodplains, and fertile valleys; red mulberry is shade-tolerant and occurs as scattered individuals in broadleaf forests along with American elm, silver maple, basswood, and yellow-poplar, among others.

**Notes:** A fast-growing, fairly short-lived tree, red mulberry is easily transplanted; the fruits are highly attractive to many birds and mammals, which disseminate the seeds. The fruit is sweet and juicy and used in jellies, jams, pies, and drinks. The wood is of little commercial value but is used locally for fence posts because it is relatively resistant to decay.

> ### In the Field
> - Leaves dull dark green, unlobed or variously lobed on the same tree, upper surface rough, underside downy
> - Broken stem or cut bark exudes milky sap
> - Fruit blackberry-like, bright red at first, turning dark purple
> - Buds dark green, angled out from twig
> - Leaf larger and less shiny, fruit larger, and bark browner than those of white mulberry; also red mulberry occurs in natural, not urban habitats

# WHITE OAK    Chêne blanc

American white oak, stave oak
*Quercus alba* L.
Fagaceae: Beech Family

**Size and Form.** White oak achieves great
size, 18 to 25 m tall and 60 to 120 cm or more
in diameter, with a short, thick trunk and
stout, horizontal, wide-spreading limbs,
gnarled in old age, and a broad, open,
rounded crown. In dense forest stands, the
trunk is long, cylindrical, and free of branches for much of its
length, supporting a narrow crown. A very deep taproot and
deep-set lateral roots render it very wind-firm.

**Leaves.** Alternate, simple, blades 12 to 20 cm long and about
half as wide; oblong, with five to nine rounded lobes; leaf
shape variable: some leaves tend to have broad lobes and
narrow sinuses, and some leaves
have narrow lobes and deep,
narrow sinuses; thin, firm, bright
green above, pale beneath,
smooth, persistent through the
winter on open-grown young
trees and sometimes on the lower
crowns of mature trees. Petiole
short, stout, 1 to 2 cm long.
Autumn color: purple-brown to
red-russet.

**Bark.** Thick, light ashy gray, highly variable in appearance;
separated into vertical scaly blocks or shallow fissures and flat-
topped ridges.

**Twigs.** Somewhat stout with light-colored pores, shiny or
covered with a whitish bloom, shoots reddish gray, turning ashy
gray.

**Buds.** Terminal bud 3 to 4 mm long, broadly oval, blunt, with
dark red-brown glabrous scales; lateral buds smaller, divergent
from twig, clustered toward tip of twig.

**Flowers.** May or June, with the leaves, monoecious. Male catkins hairy, 5 to 8 cm long; female flowers reddish, very hairy, on short stalks.

**Fruit.** Acorn, maturing in autumn of first season, sessile or short-stalked. Cup has small knob-like scales and encloses a quarter of the nut, the cup rim has no fringe. The nut is long-oval, rounded at the tip, 1.3 to 2 cm long, light brown. Germinates in autumn.

**Distribution.** White oak grows throughout most of the eastern United States, from southwestern Maine, southeastern New Hampshire, southern New England, and southernmost Quebec, west to southern Ontario, central Michigan, to southeastern Minnesota, south to East Texas, east to northern Florida and Georgia. Absent from the high mountains of the Appalachians, the Mississippi Delta, and the Gulf Coastal Plain. The largest specimens occur in Delaware and the Eastern Shore of Maryland.

**Habitat.** Most common on dry-mesic upland sites with well-drained sand-loam or clay-loam soils, usually mixed with other oaks, black cherry, hickories, sugar maple, or white pine. Moderately shade-tolerant, persists as an understory tree a long time, but grows well once the stand is opened. Slow-growing and long-lived—up to 500 or 600 years.

**Notes:** For the meaning of *Quercus,* see chestnut oak; page 116; *alba* is Latin for "white," referring to the ashy bark. White oak is an important timber species and the most important species in the white oak group (others include chestnut oak, swamp white oak, and bur oak). White oak is the state tree of Connecticut, specifically the Charter oak, which once stood in Hartford. Bubble-like structures (tyloses) form in the cell cavities of vessels in the white oak group, making the wood watertight. The sapwood is white to very light brown and the heartwood of white oaks is light to dark brown, heavy, straight-grained, hard, tough, very stiff, and strong with a coarse texture. In addition, the wood of the white oak group is very resistant to decay. Uses include wooden ships, crossties, timber bridges, dimension lumber, flooring, furniture, veneer, barrels, kegs, and casks. A desirable shade tree but difficult to transplant from the wild due to the long taproot. The acorns are a valuable source of food for wildlife—more than 180 species of birds and mammals feed on them.

> **In the Field**
> - Leaves blue-green with deep, rounded clefts between the rounded regular lobes
> - Leaves never have a large terminal lobe and are hairless on the underside
> - Lateral buds are reddish brown, rounded, and diverge from the twig
> - Acorn cap is shallow, enclosing a quarter of the nut; the rim has no fringe
> - Mature bark is light gray with thin rectangular plates on the lower trunk

# RED OAK   Chêne rouge

Northern red oak
*Quercus rubra* L.
Fagaceae: Beech Family

**Size and Form.** Red oak grows to be a
large tree, 20 to 30 m tall and 40 to 100 or
more cm in diameter. Forest-grown trees
have a long, straight trunk and relatively
few, large, spreading limbs and slender
branches. Open-grown trees have a
relatively short, thick, trunk and massive spreading branches
form a broad, round crown. The lower trunk usually is free of
dead branches.

**Leaves.** Alternate, simple, blades 13 to 23 cm long, 10 to 15 cm
wide, seven to eleven (seven to nine most common) coarse-
toothed tapering pointed lobes, each tooth tipped with a bristle;
sinuses are wide, oblique, and rounded; leaf is thin, smooth,
and firm, a dull green above, paler beneath with tufts of hair in
the vein axils. New leaves just emerging in spring are pink or

red. Petiole stout, 2 to 4 cm long.
Autumn color: leaves of young
seedlings and sprouts red; leaves of
mature trees russet-brown.

**Bark.** Smooth, gray-brown on
young trunks, thicker, darker, and
fissured into long, wide, flat,
smooth ridges (like ski trails) on
old trunks. Newly exposed inner
bark pinkish tan.

**Twigs.** Moderately stout with light-colored pores, smooth and
greenish brown, becoming dark reddish brown.

**Buds.** Terminal bud 6 mm long, oval, pointed, slightly angled,
reddish brown and smooth or slightly hairy at the tip. Lateral
buds similar but smaller, clustered toward tip of twig.

**Flowers.** May or June, when the leaves are half grown,

monoecious. Male catkins hairy, 10 to 13 cm long; female flowers on short smooth stalks, spreading, bright yellow-green.

**Fruit.** Acorn, maturing in autumn of the second season, singly or in pairs, stalkless or short-stalked, cup shallow, saucer-shaped and enclosing only the base of the nut, scales tight, glossy, bright red-brown. Nut oblong, 2 to 3 cm long with a broad base, 1.3 to 2 cm in diameter, red-brown, kernel white, very bitter.

**Distribution.** Widespread in the eastern United States, red oak occurs throughout New England, is the common oak of eastern Canada, and is the only native oak that extends to Nova Scotia. It grows from Cape Breton Island, Nova Scotia, Prince Edward Island, the Gaspé Peninsula, Quebec, western New Brunswick, and Ontario west to Minnesota, south to eastern Oklahoma, east to Arkansas, southern Alabama, Georgia, and North Carolina.

**Habitat.** In New England, Canada, and the rest of the northern part of its range, red oak grows on cool, mesic, well-drained soils, where it is commonly associated with sugar maple, beech, yellow birch, red maple, white ash, eastern white pine, eastern hemlock, and northern white-cedar. Red oak is a component in many forest types and is associated with numerous other species. It is moderately shade-tolerant.

**Notes:** For the meaning of *Quercus*, see chestnut oak, page 116; *rubra* is Latin for "red," referring to the color (sometimes) of leaf veination. Red oak, the provincial tree of Prince Edward Island, is an important timber species and the most important species in the red oak group (others include black oak, scarlet oak, and pin oak). The sapwood is white to very light brown with reddish brown heartwood. The wood is hard, heavy, strong, and stiff, with straight grain and course texture. Uses include furniture, flooring, wooden ships, crossties, timber bridges, dimension lumber, veneer, plywood, and fuel wood. Red oak is an important landscape tree; open-grown trees have broad symmetrical crowns. The acorns are a very important food for wildlife, especially deer, bears, squirrels, and jays, among many other species. Old red oaks commonly develop cavities that are important den sites for squirrels, raccoons, and other mammals.

### *In the Field*
- Leaves with seven to nine pointed lobes, each lobe wider toward the base and each tooth on the lobes ending in a bristle
- The clefts or sinuses between the lobes are more V-shaped than U-shaped
- The bark on mature trees has long ridges and shallow fissures like smooth "ski trails"; inner bark is pinkish red
- The acorn is barrel-shaped: large and wide—1.2 to 2.5 cm long and about as wide, with a very shallow, saucer-like cup with small, tight scales

# BLACK OAK   Chêne noir

Yellow bark oak
*Quercus velutina* Lam.
Fagaceae: Beech Family

**Size and Form.** Although black oak attains
large size in the southern part of its range,
in New England and Canada it is normally a
medium-sized tree, up to 25 m tall and 40 to
90 cm in diameter. The lower limbs are
horizontal and the upper ones ascending;
the crown is variable, generally spreading
and rounded but irregular. Dead branches usually are not
persistent on the lower trunk. Deeply taprooted.

**Leaves.** Alternate, simple, blades 10 to 20 cm long and 10 to 15
cm wide; five to seven-lobes, usually seven-lobed with a few

bristle-tipped teeth on each
pointed lobe. Lobes oblique or at
right angles to the mid-vein, with
parallel sides and separated by
deep U-shaped sinuses. Thick,
leathery; shiny dark green above;
yellow-brown and rough-textured
beneath, hairy early in the season,
later a few hairs remain on the
veins and in the vein axils of the
underside. Petiole stout, 3.5 to 6
cm long. Autumn color: russet.

**Bark.** Smooth and dark gray when young, thick and nearly
black, deeply furrowed with many horizontal cracks giving a
blocky appearance on mature trunks. This blocky pattern is
often visible on the lowest part of young trunks. The inner bark
is thick, yellow or orange when newly exposed, bitter.

**Twigs.** Stout with light-colored pores, at first very scaly or
hairy, later smooth, reddish brown, finally mottled gray by
autumn. Pith star-shaped in cross section.

**Buds.** Terminal bud 6 mm long, oval to conical, sharp-pointed, distinctly angled, with light gray hairs obscuring the surface of the scales; lateral buds clustered toward tip of twig.

**Flowers.** May, when the leaves are half grown, monoecious. Male flower catkins are downy, 10 to 15 cm long, flowers have yellow anthers. Female flowers reddish, on short, very hairy stalks.

**Fruit.** Acorn, maturing in autumn of the second season; stalkless or short-stalked, cup deep, bowl-shaped, enclosing about half of the nut; scales light brown, thin, loose-fitting and overlapping, square at the ends, giving the cup rim a fringed appearance. Nut oval, 1.2 to 1.8 cm long, light red-brown, often with a downy surface and striate; kernel yellow, bitter.

**Distribution.** Black oak is a common tree of the eastern United States. In New England, it is found primarily in the southern part of the region, occurring from southwestern Maine and southeastern New Hampshire to Connecticut and Rhode Island, west in scattered parts of New York to extreme southern Ontario, north of Lake Erie and Lake Ontario, and southeastern Minnesota, south to East Texas, and east to northwestern Florida and Georgia. Absent from the lower Mississippi Valley and the Gulf Coastal Plain.

**Habitat.** In southern New England, black oak grows on cool, dry-mesic upland sites, elsewhere on dry sites, typically well-drained sandy or gravelly soils. Intolerant of shade and competition, it commonly is associated with white pine, scarlet oak, shagbark hickory, and red maple.

**Notes:** For the meaning of *Quercus,* see chestnut oak, page 116; *velutina* is from the Latin *villus* (fleece) and refers to the velvety young leaves. Black oak in New England tends to be a small, sometimes scraggly tree on very dry sites. It is not an important landscape tree—the deep taproot makes transplanting difficult. The wood is similar to that of red oak and used for similar purposes (see red oak, page 138). The acorns are a valuable food source for many wildlife species including deer, bears, turkeys, squirrels, and jays, among others.

### In the Field

- Leaves dark shiny green, lobes pointed and with several bristle-tipped teeth, separated by U-shaped sinuses that are deep on "sun" leaves, shallow on "shade" leaves
- Buds are densely hairy, dull grayish brown, angled from the twig
- Mature bark almost black, separated into a blocky pattern; inner bark thick, yellow or orange, bitter
- Acorns small, half-enclosed by a bowl-shaped cap with loose, square-tipped scales along the rim

# SCARLET OAK   Chêne écarlate

Black oak, red oak, Spanish oak
*Quercus coccinea* Muenchh.
Fagaceae: Beech Family

**Size and Form.** Scarlet oak is a medium-sized tree, growing 15 to 21 m tall and 30 to 60 cm in diameter. The long trunk and spreading, slender branches form an open, rounded crown on open-grown trees and an irregular cylindrical crown on forest trees. The substantial taproot makes it very wind-firm.

**Leaves.** The alternate simple leaves have deep U-shaped sinuses and five to nine pointed lobes with three-toothed tips, the middle tooth the longest, and all ending in a bristle. The leaves are 7.5 to 15 cm long and 7 to 13 cm wide, red when they first appear, dark green above and paler beneath when fully formed. Autumn color: bright scarlet.

**Bark.** Moderately thick, dark brown to almost black, shallow fissures separate with somewhat scaly ridges.

**Twigs.** Slender with light-colored pores, new growth hairy, green, turning a smooth pale brown.

**Buds.** Broadly egg-shaped, 3 to 6 mm long, buds near the end of the twig clustered about the terminal bud, which is about 6 mm long. Buds are dark reddish brown, upper half hairy.

**Flowers.** May, when the leaves are half grown, monoecious. Male flowers in long, drooping catkins 7.5 to 10 cm long, produced from lateral buds of the previous year, or among the scales of the terminal bud. Female flowers are solitary or in twos or threes on short stalks about 1 cm long in the axils of the new leaves.

**Fruit.** Acorns borne singly or in pairs, stalkless or on short stalks, ripening at the end of the second summer. Egg-shaped, 15 to 20 mm long, light reddish brown, often with concentric rings near the tip. The cap deep, with glossy, tight, reddish brown scales, covering a third to a half of the nut; dropped in late autumn; kernel white, bitter.

**Distribution.** The native range of scarlet oak extends from southwestern Maine and central New Hampshire west to eastern New York, Ohio, southern Michigan, and Indiana, south to southern Illinois, southeastern Missouri, and central Mississippi, east to southwestern Georgia, and north along the Piedmont to North Carolina. In New England, it is restricted to the southern half of the region and is common near the coast. It is planted widely in eastern Canada as a landscape tree. Endangered in Maine.

**Habitat.** A tree of sandy soils primarily, scarlet oak also occurs on dry ridges. Shade-intolerant and fast-growing. Commonly associated with red and black oaks.

**Notes:** For the meaning of *Quercus,* see chestnut oak, page 116; *coccinea* is Latin for "scarlet," referring to the fall foliage. A widely planted ornamental and street tree for its fast growth, attractive form, and bright scarlet autumn foliage. The wood is similar to that of red oak but of lower quality and used for similar purposes (see red oak, page 138). The acorns are a valuable food source for many wildlife species including squirrels, chipmunks, mice, deer, wild turkeys, jays, and woodpeckers.

> ### In the Field
> - Leaves shiny with pointed lobes and deep, nearly round sinuses, bright scarlet in autumn
> - Upper half of buds with whitish hair
> - Acorn cap deep with reddish brown scales, enclosing a third to a half of the nut; acorn tip has concentric rings
> - Inner bark pinkish brown, not bitter

# PIN OAK    Chêne des marais

Swamp oak, water oak, swamp Spanish oak
*Quercus palustris* Muenchh.
Fagaceae: Beech Family

**Size and Form.** Pin oak is a large tree 15 to
26 m tall and 70 or more cm in diameter,
with a long trunk and a more or less conical
crown. The upper branches are ascending
and the lower branches droop; dead
branches are retained in the lower crown.

**Leaves.** Alternate, simple, 10 to 15 cm long, widest at or just
above the middle and deeply lobed with round-bottomed
irregular sinuses reaching almost to the mid-rib. The five to
nine horizontal lobes are tipped with three to four coarse

bristle-tipped teeth. The upper
edges of lobes are at right angles
to the mid-rib. Leaves smooth,
shiny and dark green above, paler
below. Petiole is slender, 2 to 5 cm
long. Autumn color: bright red.

**Bark.** Grayish brown to blackish,
relatively thin and smooth; with
age, low scaly ridges separated by
shallow fissures, inner bark pink.

**Twigs.** Slender, tough, smooth with light-colored pores, bright
reddish brown or gray-brown.

**Buds.** Terminal bud oval, pointed, about 3 mm long, light
brown, lateral buds near the twig tip clustered around the
terminal bud.

**Flowers.** May, when the leaves are about one-third developed,
monoecious. Male flowers in long drooping catkins 5 to 7.5 cm
long, produced either from the lateral buds of the previous
year, or from among the scales of the terminal bud. Female
flowers red, usually two or three together on a short stalk in the
axils of the new leaves.

**Fruit.** Acorns, ripening in autumn of second season; short-stalked or nearly sessile, singly or in pairs, almost spherical; light brown, often striate, about 12 mm long with the shallow reddish brown cup covering about a fourth of the nut. Kernel yellow, bitter.

**Distribution.** Pin oak grows from the Connecticut River Valley in Massachusetts south to southwestern Connecticut, the Hudson River Valley in New York west through central Pennsylvania and extreme southern Ontario to northern Illinois, Iowa south to eastern Kansas, and east to Virginia. Disjunct populations occur in western Vermont, central Massachusetts, and southern Rhode Island.

**Habitat.** Pin oak is a tree of poorly drained soils in swamps and along streams, yet flourishes when planted in dry upland sites. It is intolerant of shade; it is widely planted as a street tree.

**Notes:** For the meaning of *Quercus,* see chestnut oak, page 116; *palustris* is Latin for "of swamps or wet places." Fast-growing and moderately long-lived, pin oak often attains very large size as a planted specimen. The tiny branches from a distance give the appearance of the tree being full of pins, but the name apparently comes from the many pin knots in the wood caused by the numerous persistent dead branches. The wood is similar to that of red oak but of lower quality and used for similar purposes (see red oak, page 138). Easily transplanted, pin oak is an important landscape tree because of its symmetrical form and bright red fall foliage. Pin oak acorns dropped near water are an important food for wood ducks, opossum, and many other species.

### *In the Field*

- Small leaves with narrow, horizontal pointed lobes and very deep, round sinuses
- Smooth, small buds
- Bark lacks deep furrows
- Acorn is very small, nearly spherical; cap is shallow
- The lower live branches droop and numerous dead lower branches are persistent
- Occurs on flat, poorly drained sites and swamps and dry sites when planted; planted specimens common as street or landscape trees

# POST OAK

Iron Oak
*Quercus stellata* Wangenh.
Fagaceae: Beech Family

**Size and Form.** Post oak is a medium-sized
southern tree, 15 to 18 m tall and 30 to 60 cm
in diameter, with a dense, rounded crown
and stout spreading branches. It is slow-
growing in comparison to other oaks.

**Leaves.** Alternate, simple, blades 10 to 15 cm
long, 7.5 to 10 cm wide, normally five-lobed; the two middle
lobes are more or less square and opposite, giving the leaf a
shape resembling a Maltese cross, dark green with scattered
star-like tufts of hairs above,
tawny and densely hairy below.
Autumn color: russet.

**Bark.** Similar to that of white oak
but more reddish brown and
more definite longitudinal ridges.

**Twigs.** Stout, pubescent with
light-colored pores, yellowish
gray, becoming dark brown.

**Buds.** More or less covered with dense matted hair. Terminal
bud 2 to 3 mm long, spherical or broadly oval, covered with
brown, hairy scales, lateral buds similar but smaller.

**Flowers.** April to May in New England, with the leaves,
monoecious. Male flowers are borne in pendent catkins 5 to 10
cm long, female flowers are sessile or short-stalked and
inconspicuous.

**Fruit.** Acorns, mature in one growing season, and drop soon
after ripening in autumn. Acorns stalkless or short-stalked,
either solitary, in pairs, or small clusters; oval or long-oval,
broad at the base, 13 to 19 mm long, striate, the cup covering a
third to a half the length of the nut. The cup is bowl-shaped,

**Simple, Lobed, Alternate   149**

pale, often pubescent inside, hairy outside, with tight reddish scales.

**Distribution.** Post oak extends from southeastern Massachusetts (including Cape Cod and the Islands), Rhode Island, southern Connecticut, and extreme southeastern New York (including Long Island) south and west through southeastern Pennsylvania, Missouri, east Texas, and central Florida. Absent from the lower Mississippi Valley and Delta and the Texas Gulf Coast.

**Habitat.** Post oak in New England, the scruffy sand post oak (*Q. stellata* var. *margaretta* (Ashe) Sarg.) variety, grows on deep, dry, sandy, or coarse-textured nutrient-poor soils with low organic matter. It commonly is found in association with pitch pine and scrub oak. Intolerant of shade.

**Notes:** For the meaning of *Quercus,* see chestnut oak, page 116; *stellata* is Latin for "starred," referring to the star-like tuffs of hair on the leaves. Like others in the white oak group, post oak acorns are readily consumed by wildlife, especially deer, turkeys, jays, and a variety of other birds, and squirrels and small rodents. Good seed crops occur every two to three years. Post oak makes a beautiful shade tree, and commonly is planted as an ornamental. The wood is similar to that of white oak and used for similar purposes (see white oak, page 135). Its common name comes from use as fence posts because of its resistance to decay.

> ### In the Field
> - Leaves cross-shaped with square middle lobes
> - Stout, hairy twigs
> - Bark similar to white oak but with more pronounced vertical ridges, often appearing twisted along the trunk
> - Acorns striate

# BUR OAK    Chêne à gros fruits

Mossycup oak
*Quercus macrocarpa* Michx.
Fagaceae: Beech Family

**Size and Form.** Bur oak in deep soil grows
to be a large tree, 18 to 25 m tall and 60 to
120 cm in diameter, with a rounded,
spreading crown similar to that of white
oak. On exposed shallow soils in Canada
and New England, it is usually a small,
stunted tree 15 m tall with a short trunk and gnarled branches.
Epicormic branches often occur along the trunk. Bur oak has a
wide-spreading root system with a deep taproot.

**Leaves.** Alternate, simple, blades 15 to 30 cm long, 7.5 to 15 cm
wide, lobed but shape variable on the same tree—some leaves
have seven to nine rounded lobes, others (at least one per
shoot) with an unlobed, wavy-
toothed portion at the apex above
two deep sinuses, and others
resemble white oak. Upper
surface shiny green, paler and
hairy beneath. Petiole 16 to 25 mm
long. Autumn color: russet.

**Bark.** Thick, rough, gray-brown,
becoming deeply furrowed with
irregular scaly ridges with age.

**Twigs.** Stout, yellow-brown, hairy, becoming gray-brown, often
with corky ridges.

**Buds.** Terminal bud 3 to 6 mm long, broadly oval or conical,
pale reddish brown, somewhat hairy; lateral buds pressed
against the twig.

**Flowers.** May to June, with the leaves, monoecious. Male
catkins slender, hairy, 10 to 15 cm long. Female flowers stalkless
or short-stalked, reddish, very hairy.

**Simple, Lobed, Alternate    151**

**Fruit.** Acorn, ripens autumn of first season; sessile or short-stalked, variable in size and shape but cup typically deep and conspicuously fringed at the rim, enclosing at least half the nut; nut 2 to 4 cm long, oval to oblong, brownish, downy at the apex, kernel white, sweet. Germinates in autumn.

**Distribution.** Bur oak is distributed widely in the eastern United States and is the most common of the native white oaks in Canada. It occurs in disjunct populations from New Brunswick in the St. John River drainage, Maine in the Penobscot River drainage, New York, Connecticut, and west in contiguous range from southern Quebec and Ontario to central Manitoba and eastern Saskatchewan south to east Texas, Arkansas, central Tennessee, and West Virginia.

**Habitat.** Best growth (and largest trees) occur on deep, rich bottomland soils; also occurs on upland limestone soils. Stunted specimens on shallow soils overlaying granite bedrock occur at the northern limits of its range. Bur oak is drought-tolerant and fairly shade-tolerant, and fire-resistant due to its thick bark, which accounts for its invasion of prairies or grasslands.

**Notes:** For the meaning of *Quercus,* see chestnut oak, page 116; *macrocarpa* means "large fruit," from the Greek *macros* (large) and *karpos* (fruit). The wood is similar to that of white oak and used for similar purposes (see white oak, page 135). Bur oak hybridizes with swamp white oak, with which it commonly occurs. It transplants well despite its taproot and is tolerant of city conditions. The acorns are consumed by many wildlife species.

---

### In the Field
- Leaf shape highly variable on same tree—top of leaf broad, base narrow, at least one leaf per shoot unlobed with a broad wavy-toothed upper half
- Leaf underside hairy
- Lateral buds pressed against the twig
- Thick gray-brown bark with irregular fissures and scaly ridges
- Twigs stout with corky ridges
- Acorn cap rim has conspicuous fringe

# AMERICAN SYCAMORE  Platane occidental

American planetree, buttonwood, button-ball tree
*Platanus occidentalis* L.
Platanacae: Sycamore Family

**Size and Form.** American sycamore is one of
the largest of eastern hardwood trees, up to 35
m tall, 100 to 200 cm in diameter. The trunk is
massive, forming a broad, open, irregular
crown of large, crooked, spreading branches.

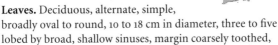

**Leaves.** Deciduous, alternate, simple,
broadly oval to round, 10 to 18 cm in diameter, three to five
lobed by broad, shallow sinuses, margin coarsely toothed,

base wedge-shaped to deeply
indented. Leaf stipules
prominent in the spring. Leaves
are bright green above, hairless,
paler below with woolly white
hair on the main veins; petiole
densely hairy, hollow at the base
and completely enclosing the
bud. Autumn color: yellow to
brown.

**Bark.** On young trees at first brownish; soon becoming mottled
brown and white by the shedding of the outer bark in large,
irregular, thin pieces, exposing the lighter, creamy white inner
layers; often entirely brown and scaly at the base of older trees.
The bark is characteristic of the species and can be identified at
a great distance.

**Twigs.** Moderately slender, zigzag, dark orange-brown,
smooth. Stipule scars are narrow and encircle the twig.

**Buds.** End and lateral buds are cone-shaped, blunt, 6 to 10 mm
long, divergent, resinous, with a single cap-like scale. Terminal
bud absent. Leaf scars are narrow and encircle the bud.

**Flowers.** May with the leaves, monoecious. Male flowers are
small, dark red, in clusters along the twigs; female flowers are

green tinged with red, in ball-like clusters on long stalks near the shoot tips.

**Fruit.** A ball-shaped, brown, aggregate head, 2 to 3 cm in diameter, on an 8 to 16 cm long stalk; individual fruit is a small, one-seeded nutlet, elongated, with stiff brownish hairs at the base that spread apart when the aggregate breaks up. Persist on the branches through the winter into the following spring, gradually dispersing seed.

**Distribution.** American sycamore occurs throughout southern New England, with disjunct populations in southwestern Maine, into New Hampshire and Vermont in major southern river valleys, and the Champlain Valley in Vermont. Widely distributed in the southern United States from southern New England to Iowa, south to Texas and east to Georgia. In Canada, it grows in extreme southern Ontario.

**Habitat.** Grows along riverbanks and on rich, moist bottomlands as scattered individuals or small groups in mixtures with other hardwood trees. Associates include river birch, eastern cottonwood, red maple, silver maple, black willow, boxelder, American elm, red ash, black ash.

**Notes:** The botanical name is from the Greek *platus*, meaning "broad" in reference to the broad leaves. American sycamore is shade-intolerant, fast-growing, and long-lived. It is of secondary importance as a timber tree because it is not widely available. The heartwood is light to dark brown, close-textured, with interlocked grain, and is moderate in most physical characteristics. Uses include furniture, especially drawer sides, containers, millwork, flooring, veneer, pallets, boxes, plywood, pulpwood, and particleboard. Radial surfaces, such as in quarter-sawn boards, display a striking ray fleck pattern. Sycamore is occasionally planted as an ornamental but London planetree, a hybrid (*Platanus* x *acerifolia* (Ait.) Willd.), is more often planted because it is more tolerant of urban conditions and more resistant to anthracnose, a fungus that defoliates American sycamore. More recently, because of its rapid growth, sycamore has become a favored species for intensively cultivated biomass farms in the southeastern United States.

### In the Field
- Mottled brown and white bark
- Large, broad leaves, with three to five coarsely toothed lobes, separated by shallow, broad sinuses
- Buds cone-shaped, blunt, with a single cap-like scale, covered entirely by leaf petiole
- Fruit heads ball-shaped, dense, brown, long-stalked, borne singly, persist on twigs

# Group 10
## Simple, Lobed, Opposite

## BLACK MAPLE  Érable noir

Black sugar maple, hard maple, rock maple
*Acer nigrum* Michx. f.
Aceraceae: Maple Family

**Size and Form.** Black maple is a large tree, 18 to 24 m tall and up to 100 cm in diameter. Its stout branches form a wide, round crown in the open; in the forest, the trunk is long and columnar with a shallow, flat-topped crown.

**Leaves.** Opposite, simple, three-lobed, less commonly five-lobed with the lower two additional lobes small; usually wider than long; margins smooth, sides of larger leaves commonly drooping; thick, firm; hairless, dark green above, yellow-green and densely pubescent beneath; petiole stout, hairy, 8 to 12 cm long with paired leafy appendages at leaf base (see sugar maple, page 159). Autumn color: yellow or yellow-brown, seldom red or orange like sugar maple.

**Bark.** Moderately thick, deeply furrowed into long, dark gray or blackish ridges.

**Twigs.** Fairly stout, smooth, yellow-brown, usually hairy, with prominent dots of corky pores.

**Buds.** Small, oval, pointed, with dark red-brown, downy scales.

**Flowers.** April to May, with the leaves; in almost sessile flat-topped or somewhat rounded clusters, yellowish-green, about 6 mm long, on pendulous hairy stalks about 3 to 7 cm long. Polygamous.

**Fruit.** Paired samaras; ripen in autumn, borne on slender stems, with divergent wings, indistinguishable from sugar maple.

**Distribution.** Black maple is uncommon in the region. Closely related and similar to sugar maple (*A. saccharum*); extends further west but not as far north or northeast as sugar maple. It is sometimes planted as an ornamental. It extends from New England (locally in northwestern Vermont, southwestern New Hampshire, western Massachusetts, northwestern Connecticut), New York, and southern Quebec west and south through southern Ontario, southeastern Minnesota, northeastern Kansas, and western North Carolina, local in New Jersey and Maryland.

**Habitat.** Black maple grows on a variety of soils but is most common on moist soils of river floodplains and bottomlands in mixed hardwood forests—wetter sites than those where sugar maple grows best. Associated trees on such sites include American elm, silver maple, basswood, and red ash. On drier sites, common associates include American beech, yellow-poplar, sugar maple, northern red oak, white ash, and eastern hemlock.

**Notes:** For the meaning of *Acer,* see sugar maple, page ooo. Once considered to be a variety of sugar maple, black maple is considered a relict species of an earlier warmer, drier climatic era; trees with intermediate features commonly occur because it hybridizes readily with sugar maple. The wood is similar in quality and uses to sugar maple—it is hard, heavy, strong, close-grained, and cream-colored. Like sugar maple, black maple can be tapped for sap for making maple syrup. Black maple is shade-tolerant and long-lived. Ruffed grouse, wild turkeys, and many small birds eat the seed. Squirrels and chipmunks cache the seeds after removing the husk and wing.

### In the Field

- Leaves large, normally with three pointed lobes, the side lobes drooping, and the leaf underside and petiole hairy
- Buds resemble a sharpened pencil, scales generally hairy
- Bark black with long, narrow, vertical ridges
- Sugar maple has five-lobed smaller leaves that do not droop, the middle lobe with parallel margins, no leaf-like appendages at the stem base, and the leaf underside and petiole are not hairy

# SUGAR MAPLE    Érable à sucre

Rock maple, hard maple
*Acer saccharum* Marsh.
Aceraceae: Maple Family

**Size and Form.** Sugar maple is a stately tree, commonly attaining a height of 30 m and a trunk diameter of 60 to 120 cm. Under forest conditions, develops a clear, straight trunk; when open-grown, develops stout branches near the ground and a spreading, rounded crown with a fine branching pattern.

**Leaves.** Opposite, simple, 7 to 13 cm long and wide, normally five-lobed (rarely three-lobed), margin of lobes smooth or somewhat wavy-toothed, lobe tips tapering to point, leaf base heart-shaped, surfaces smooth, bright green above, paler below. Autumn color: golden yellow with variable amounts of orange and red.

**Bark.** Gray, on mature trees deeply furrowed with long, irregular thick plates or ridges with curly edges, occasionally scaly, highly variable. Smooth on young trees.

**Twigs.** Slender, smooth, glossy tan or brownish, pith white, leaf scars V-shaped, with three vein scars.

**Buds.** Terminal bud 6 to 9 mm long, conical, acute, sharply pointed, reddish to dark brown with four to eight pairs of scales: lateral buds similar but smaller, pressed against the twig.

**Flowers.** April to May, before the leaves, small, yellow, most flowers perfect but normally only the male or female parts functional; long-stalked, in drooping clusters over the entire crown. Polygamous.

**Fruit.** Paired samaras; ripen in autumn, sometimes persistent to December, borne on slender stems, U-shaped with divergent wings, about 25 mm long. Germinate the following spring. Fruiting begins on forest trees when about 40 years old, with good crops every three to seven years and light crops in intervening years. The ideal temperature for seed germination is 34 degrees Fahrenheit, the lowest known for any forest tree.

**Distribution.** Found throughout New England and adjacent Canada. Range extends from Quebec, all of New Brunswick, Nova Scotia, west to southeastern Manitoba south to Arkansas and southern New Jersey, and through the Appalachian Mountains to Georgia.

**Habitat.** Commonly deep, rich, moist soils of upland forests or fields; best development occurs on loamy soils with pH range of 5.5 to 7.3. Sugar maple grows on a wide variety of sites, but does not grow well on dry, shallow soils and rarely, if ever, found in swamps. In New England commonly occurs on sites with abundant organic matter. Once rooted, sugar maple seedlings can tolerate dense shade for many years, waiting for an opening in the canopy so they can develop further. In the forest, sugar maple commonly is associated with American beech, yellow birch, red maple, aspen, northern red oak, red spruce, white pine, and hemlock in New England, and less frequently with many other tree species throughout its range.

**Notes:** *Acer* is from the Celtic *ac* for "hard" in reference to the wood; *saccharum,* meaning "sweet" or "sugary," and referring to the sap, is from the Sanskrit *sarkara,* "sugar" or "grit." Sugar maple, the national tree of Canada and the state tree of Vermont, is one of the most valuable timber species in eastern North America. The wood is known in the lumber trade as hard maple and is prized for its hardness, strength, working and finishing qualities, fine grain, and light color. Uses include flooring, furniture, interior finish and cabinets, and veneer (especially curly, wavy, and bird's-eye figures). It also has been used in turned products, toys, musical instruments, and sporting goods, such as bowling pins and croquet mallets and balls. Maple sap is collected by tapping trees in very early spring and boiling it down to produce maple syrup and sugar. The ratio of sap to syrup is 40 to 1 and requires about five taps to produce a gallon of syrup. It is generally accepted that the

Native Americans in northeastern North America discovered production of maple sugar from maple sap and the process was improved and refined after the arrival of Europeans. New England has been a major producer of maple syrup and today accounts for half of U.S. production. Quebec is the largest producer of maple syrup in the world. Many birds and small mammals eat the seed. Large, old sugar maples commonly develop cavities that serve as valuable den trees that stand for many years.

*In the Field*
- Leaves five-lobed, central lobe somewhat square, with parallel sides
- Terminal bud conical, sharp-pointed, overlapping scales smooth
- Bark on old trees has large plates curving away from trunk along their sides
- Paired samaras have divergent wings

# RED MAPLE   Érable rouge

Swamp maple, soft maple
*Acer rubrum* L.
Aceraceae: Maple Family

**Size and Form.** Red maple is normally a
medium-sized tree, 15 to 20 m high and 50
to 80 cm in diameter; occasionally, open-
grown individuals reach great size with
massive trunks, although their heights are
usually less than 25 m. In the forest, red
maple has a thrifty form, the trunk free of
branches for half or more of its length, and small upright
branches form a narrow, rounded crown.

**Leaves.** Opposite, simple, 7 to 12
cm long and wide, normally
three-lobed (occasionally five-
lobed) with broad shallow
sinuses; terminal lobe
approximately half the length of
the leaf; margins toothed or
doubly toothed; smooth green
above, whitish green beneath;
petiole long and slender. Autumn
color: bright red, orange, or
yellow.

**Bark.** On young trees smooth, light to medium gray; on mature
trees dark gray, ridged, separating into long, narrow platy
scales.

**Twigs.** Red or dark red, shiny, becoming smooth and light gray
on the branches; pith pink; not malodorous when broken (see
silver maple, page 165).

**Buds.** Dark red, terminal buds 3 to 4 mm long, blunt or
rounded, three or four pairs of scales; lateral buds similar but
smaller; flower buds numerous, usually on either side of the
leaf buds in stalkless clusters.

**Flowers.** March to May, well before the leaves; conspicuous, in compact clusters on twigs of the previous year; female flowers red, male orange, with four or five very small sepals and petals; polygamo-dioecious.

**Fruit.** Paired samaras; April to June; small, on drooping stalks, 5 to 10 cm long, wings divergent. Germinate soon after falling.

**Distribution.** Red maple is one of the most abundant and widespread trees in eastern North America, occurring throughout New England and adjacent Canada. It is found throughout all regions east of the ninety-fifth meridian, but is absent from the Prairie Peninsula of the Midwest, the coastal prairie of southern Louisiana and southeastern Texas, and the swamp prairie of the Florida Everglades.

**Habitat.** Red maple likely grows on a wider range of sites than any other forest species in North America—a wide array of soil types, textures, moisture regimes, and elevations from dry sites to swamps. Red maple is associated with many forest types, the red oak–white pine–red maple type is common on somewhat dry sites in central New England. It is a common component of sugar maple–beech–yellow birch in northern hardwoods, and of black ash–American elm–red maple in riparian areas; along swamp borders it occurs in almost pure stands. Readily colonizes upland sites; shade-tolerant and fast-growing. The abundance of red maple has increased markedly due to forest clearing and subsequent abandonment and to fire control.

**Notes:** The word *rubrum* is Latin for "red" and refers to the color of the twigs, flowers, and autumn leaves. Red maple is the state tree of Rhode Island. Red maple, silver maple, and boxelder are soft maples as opposed to sugar and black maples, which are hard maples. The wood of soft maples is similar to hard maple but is not as heavy, hard, or strong. The heartwood of red maple is creamy white to light reddish brown, usually with a grayish cast or streaks; sapwood is wide and creamy white. It is used primarily for boxes and crates, although high-grade lumber is used for some furniture. Maple syrup can be made from the sap of red maple and the other soft maples. Red maple sprouts readily and prolifically when cut; stump sprouts are browsed readily by deer. Red maple is among the first trees to flower in the spring; flowers are striking when viewed close up. Widely planted because of its flowers, red twigs, and brilliant fall foliage.

> ### In the Field
> - Leaves opposite, with three main lobes and V-shaped sinuses between lobes, leaf margins toothed or doubly toothed, dark above and light below
> - Twigs red, glossy
> - Buds small, blunt-tipped, often in large clusters, red
> - Paired samaras small and reddish, wings divergent, shed in late spring
> - Distinguished from silver maple by broader, shallower leaf sinuses, lobes of about equal size, leaves greenish white on underside, twigs shiny red, and much smaller fruits, which mature about the same time (see silver maple, page 165).

# SILVER MAPLE    Érable argenté

White maple, river maple, water maple
*Acer saccharinum* L.
Aceraceae: Maple Family

**Size and Form.** Silver maple is a fast-
growing, short-lived, medium-sized to
large tree, 20 to 35 m tall and 60 to 120 cm
in diameter. It naturally occurs on flood
plains in New England and on streambanks
and lakeshores elsewhere within its range.
In flood plain forests, silver maples develop
massive trunks that reach considerable height before
branching. Silver maple commonly is planted as an
ornamental or street tree. In these situations, the trunk is
short, commonly branching into separate stems close to the
ground, with ascending branches bending downward with the
tips upturned, and the wide-spread crown appears feathery in
winter.

**Leaves.** Opposite, simple, about 8 to 15 cm in length and width;
normally five-lobed with deep sinuses extending almost to the
mid-rib, the sides of middle lobe diverging, the terminal lobe

more than half the blade length;
the lobes themselves usually lobed,
sharply toothed; smooth and light
green above, silvery white beneath;
petioles long, slender, and
drooping. Autumn color: pale
green or yellow.

**Bark.** On young trunks, bark is
smooth, thin, light gray; on old
trunks, dark gray, somewhat
furrowed with thin scaly plates
that are free on both sides and so commonly flake off.

**Twigs.** Slender, smooth, bright reddish brown, glossy;
malodorous when broken or scraped to expose inner bark; pith
pink.

**Simple, Lobed, Opposite    165**

**Buds.** Blunt and rounded, dark red; terminal bud about 6 mm long; smooth, with bud scales ending in short-pointed tips at the bud tip; flower buds usually clustered on both sides of lateral leaf buds, globe-shaped and more conspicuous than the leaf buds.

**Flowers.** March to April, before the leaves; small, yellow-green; in stalkless radial clusters; dioecious or polygamo-monoecious. The earliest-blooming maple in North America.

**Fruit.** Paired samaras; ripen April to May, with wings widely diverging, 3 to 6 cm long, germinating soon after falling; sometimes only one seed of the pair is mature. Fruit is produced in abundance annually; silver maple samaras are the longest of any maple in North America.

**Distribution.** Silver maple occurs throughout most of New England. It is uncommon in northern and eastern Maine and absent from Cape Cod, southeastern Massachusetts, and coastal Rhode Island and Connecticut. Natural range extends from New Brunswick and southern Quebec, southeastern and southwestern Ontario, west to South Dakota, and south to Louisiana and central Georgia. Absent at higher elevations in the Appalachian Mountains and from the Atlantic coastal plains.

**Habitat.** River flood plains, streambanks, lakeshores; best growth occurs on deep, stone-free, well-drained alluvial soils, but sometimes found in muck soils of backwaters or swamps. Tolerates periodic flooding and silting. Commonly associated trees in New England include red maple, black gum, eastern cottonwood. Silver maple and American elm form a distinct riparian forest cover-type.

**Notes:** The species name *saccharinum* means "sweet" or "sugary," referring to the sap; apparently an error by Linnaeus who mistook it for sugar maple. The wood is pale brown, hard, and close-grained, but rather brittle; the thick sapwood is creamy white. A secondary timber species, it is a soft maple and sold with red maple for furniture, boxes, and crates. The branches are especially brittle and break off in storms. Though widely planted as a street tree, branch litter and shallow roots that damage sidewalks and clog drains cause problems in urban and residential settings. Several horticultural varieties for ornamental planting have been developed with deeply cut leaves or different branching habits. The buds of silver maple are an important late-winter food for red squirrels and gray squirrels and the inner bark is a food source for beaver. Large riparian trees with cavities commonly are used as nest sites by wood ducks and other hole-nesting birds.

### In the Field
- Leaves opposite, five-lobed and doubly toothed with deep narrow sinuses extending almost to the mid-rib; terminal lobe more than half the blade length; under-surface silvery white
- Paired samaras large with wings diverging almost at a right angle, and much larger than red maple
- Twigs a bright chestnut brown; inner bark malodorous
- Bark light or silver gray with thin, narrow, scaly plates
- Naturally occurring on wet sites (red maple can occur naturally on wet or dry sites)

## MOUNTAIN MAPLE    Érable à épis

White maple, whitewood, dwarf maple
*Acer spicatum* Lam.
Aceraceae: Maple Family

**Size and Form.** Mountain maple is a slow-
growing, small, bushy understory tree or
tall shrub, 5 to 6 m tall and 8 to 15 cm in
diameter. The trunk is short, crooked, and
irregularly divided into several upright,
slender limbs. The crown is open and
unevenly rounded or straggling. Mountain
maple is a common understory tree in New England and
eastern Canada.

**Leaves.** Opposite, simple, blades 6 to 12 cm long, 4 to 8 cm
wide; three-lobed above the middle, sometimes five-lobed with
the lower two lobes fairly indistinct, the lobes irregularly
toothed with sinuses wide-angled; thin, green or yellow-green,

downy, and whitish beneath; veins
prominent. Petiole slender,
reddish, and long, sometimes
longer than the blade, with
enlarged base. Autumn color: red,
orange, or yellow.

**Bark.** Thin, dull, reddish—or
grayish brown, smooth or slightly
furrowed, often with light gray or
tan blotches.

**Twigs.** Slender, yellow-green to red-green; downy, the short
gray hairs giving a dull, velvety look, especially near the tip.
Pith brown.

**Buds.** Small, somewhat flattened, pointed, bright red,
somewhat hairy, terminal bud slightly stalked, 3 to 5 mm long,
containing the flowers; one pair of non-overlapping bud scales.

**Flowers.** Late May to June, after the leaves are fully grown;
10 mm across, yellow-green to creamy white, in erect

many-flowered, long-stemmed terminal stalks; polygamo-monoecious.

**Fruit.** Paired samaras; ripen July to August, wings 10 to 15 cm long, slightly divergent, bright red, turning yellow as summer wanes and then brown in autumn; often remaining on the tree in winter; seed case indented on one side.

**Distribution.** Found throughout northern New England and adjacent Canada and in western Massachusetts and Connecticut. Native range is from Newfoundland west through Nova Scotia, New Brunswick, southern Quebec and Ontario, into Manitoba and eastern Saskatchewan; in the United States from northern Minnesota, east from Wisconsin to Maine, and south in the Appalachians into Tennessee.

**Habitat.** Well-drained, cool, moist soils along streams, in ravines, and on protected moist rocky slopes. Shade-tolerant, seldom thrives in the open. Commonly remaining on cutover sites in northern forests but soon overtopped by developing stands.

**Notes:** The species name *spicatum* means "spiked" or "spike-like," referring to the erect, long-stemmed flower clusters. After leaf-fall, mountain maple resembles alternate-leaf dogwood (which has leaf scars alternate), but the samaras and pubescent twigs identify it as a maple. Flowers and autumn foliage are quite attractive but due to its poor survival in the open it is not normally used as an ornamental.

### In the Field
- Understory shrub or small tree
- Leaves three-lobed above the middle, coarsely and irregularly toothed, thin with prominent veins, downy white on the undersurface
- Buds stalked, with two non-overlapping bud scales
- Twigs velvety, reddish

## STRIPED MAPLE    Érable de Pennsylvanie

Moosewood, moose maple.
*Acer pensylvanicum* L.
Aceraceae: Maple Family

**Size and Form.** Striped maple is a small
tree or large understory shrub, rarely more
than 9 m tall and 12 to 20 cm in diameter.
The trunk is short, dividing into upright
branches. The crown is broad and
unevenly rounded or flat-topped.

**Leaves.** Opposite, simple, large, 12 to 18 cm long and about as wide;
fully grown leaves with three short, tapering lobes on the upper
half with long fine tips pointing forward; the larger end lobe
triangular; the base rounded or somewhat heart-shaped; margins
doubly toothed; upper and lower surfaces yellow-green or

somewhat paler beneath; petiole 3
to 8 cm long, stout, grooved.
Autumn color: pale yellow.

**Bark.** Smooth, thin, initially
bright green or green-brown on
young stems, becoming
conspicuously marked with long,
thin white stripes after two to
three years; on older trunks, the
bark becomes greenish brown
with somewhat darker stripes.

**Twigs.** Moderately stout, especially for a maple, smooth, shiny
light green or reddish brown with small white lines developing
the second season, not hairy.

**Buds.** Bright red, terminal bud stalked, about 1 cm long, about
twice as long as wide, with one pair of non-overlapping scales;
hairless; lateral buds much smaller, pressed against the twig.

**Flowers.** May to June, when the leaves are about full grown;
large, 6 mm across, bell-shaped with five yellow or greenish
yellow petals, in drooping narrow clusters with a single axis 10

to 15 cm long. Trees usually monoecious, may be dioecious, or may differ in expression from one year to the next. A tree may bear only seed flowers one year and only pollen flowers the next.

**Fruit.** Paired samaras; wings about 2 cm long; divergent. Borne in long drooping clusters in summer, maturing in autumn; seed case indented on one side.

**Distribution.** In New England, striped maple occurs throughout Maine, New Hampshire, and Vermont, south to central and western Massachusetts and northwestern Connecticut. Its distribution in the region is very similar to that of mountain maple. Natural range extends from Nova Scotia and the Gaspé Peninsula of Quebec, west to southern Ontario and eastern Minnesota, south to Pennsylvania, and down the Appalachian Mountains to northern Georgia.

**Habitat.** Characteristic of mesic deciduous forest understories. Grows best on well-drained, cool, moist soils in valleys and north slopes. Very shade-tolerant. Commonly found in northern hardwood forests; associated overstory trees include sugar maple, yellow birch, northern red oak, American beech, red spruce, paper birch, eastern hemlock, and white pine. Pin cherry is the most commonly associated understory tree in northern forests.

**Notes:** The wood is not commercially important. Striped maple is slow-growing and short-lived, although specimens 100 years old have been reported. Readily browsed by moose and deer, hence the common Canadian name "moosewood" or "moose maple." With hobblebush, the large, soft leaves of striped maple cause hikers to value this "toilet paper tree."

### In the Field
- Leaves large, three-lobed above the middle, margins doubly toothed
- Bark with conspicuous vertical greenish white stripes
- Terminal bud stalked with two non-overlapping scales
- Occurs as a small understory tree or large shrub

# NORWAY MAPLE   Érable de Norvège

*Acer platanoides* L.
Aceraceae: Maple Family

**Size and Form.** Norway maple is a medium-sized, fast-growing tree, 12 to 18 m tall and 30 to 60 cm in diameter. Forms a rounded, dense, spreading crown with stout, symmetrically arranged horizontal branches, somewhat resembling that of sugar maple.

**Leaves.** Opposite, simple, 12 to 18 cm long and wide, normally five-lobed, occasionally seven-lobed, separated by rounded, wide sinuses, lobes sparingly toothed, the teeth narrow-tipped; thin, firm, bright green on both surfaces, upper surface sometimes darker green; petiole long, slender, exude a milky sap when cut or plucked from twig. Autumn color: remain green after other maples turn color, eventually turning pale yellow or orange-brown before falling two or more weeks after those of native maples.

**Bark.** Moderately thin, even on mature trees; dark gray; becoming closely fissured with low, shallow, intersecting irregular ridges. Normally not scaly or platy.

**Twigs.** Stout, smooth, shiny light brown or green-brown, same color as the buds; pores prominent. Branch tips often forked as a result of a terminal flower cluster the previous year. Opposite leaf scars almost meet around the twig.

**Buds.** Terminal bud yellow-green or dull red-brown, 6 mm or more long, plump, blunt, with two to three pairs of keeled bud scales; lateral buds small, pressed against the twig.

**Flowers.** In May or June, before or with the leaves; large, 5 to 10 mm across, greenish-yellow, in fairly erect terminal or more commonly, lateral flat clusters; usually dioecious.

**Fruit.** Paired samaras; wings 4 to 5 cm long, widely diverging wings to almost 180 degrees; seed cavity flattened; exude milky sap when separated. Ripen in autumn and germinate the following spring.

**Distribution.** Native in Europe and western Asia, so named because it was thought to have been introduced into England from Norway. A widely planted street tree in eastern North America. In New England planted, throughout Massachusetts, Connecticut, and Rhode Island, also southern New Hampshire and locally in Vermont and mid-coast Maine, and in adjacent Canada.

**Habitat.** Grows best in fertile, well-drained soils, but also grows on a wide variety of soils and disturbed sites. Becoming naturalized, often forming thickets on disturbed sites near urban areas and along roadways.

**Notes:** The word *platanoides* is from the Greek and means "resembling a plane tree." The wood is heavy, hard, and close-grained, cream-colored or light brown with white sapwood, similar to red maple, a native soft maple. Figured Norway maple is used to make violins. Norway maple is used widely for street planting because of its tolerance of harsh urban planting sites and pollution, its hardiness, and relative freedom from insect pests and diseases. Various cultivars with red or purple leaves are popular lawn and park trees, although its shallow, spreading root system and dense shade make it difficult to maintain turf beneath the trees. Because of its extreme tolerance of shade and prolific seed production, it invades local woodlands, replacing native shrubs and trees.

> *In the Field*
> - Leaves opposite, broad, with five to seven lobes; petioles exude a milky sap when cut
> - Terminal buds large, blunt, smooth
> - Paired samaras large with wide-spread wings with milky sap when separated
> - Bark dark gray to blackish with regular, tight, narrow, interlacing ridges
> - Crown wider than tall on open-grown trees

## AMERICAN MOUNTAIN-ASH    Sorbier d'Amérique

Dogberry
*Sorbus americana* Marsh.
Rosaceae: Rose Family

**Size and Form.** American mountain-ash
is a small tree or shrub, up to 15 m tall. The
trunk is short with spreading, slender
branches forming a narrow, rounded
crown. Often multiple trunks from root
suckers give it a shrub-like appearance.

**Leaves.** Deciduous, alternate, odd-pinnately compound, 15 to
25 cm long with paired leaflets on short stalks, end leaflet

stalked; thirteen to seventeen
leaflets 5 to 8 cm long, with
serrated margins, sharply
pointed, smooth, light green
above and paler below. Autumn
color: yellow.

**Bark.** Thin, light gray, smooth,
and looks somewhat like that of
apple, except for conspicuous
elongated horizontal pores. Scaly
patches develop with age. Inner
bark fragrant.

**Twigs.** Stout, smooth, grayish to reddish brown, and covered
with a faint waxy bloom.

**Buds.** Terminal buds are pointed and red, slightly curved,
about 6 to 12 cm long, sticky, with hairy inner scales.

**Flowers.** Late May to early June when leaves are fully grown; white, perfect, borne in broad, flat clusters 7.5 to 10 cm across.

**Fruit.** A berry-like pome, bright orange-red, 4 to 6 mm across. It ripens in autumn and is persistent until spring.

**Distribution.** Found throughout northern New England and adjacent Canada. In southern New England, found in Western Massachusetts and extreme northwestern Connecticut.

**Habitat.** Mountain-ash is found in thin, rocky soils at higher elevations where it occurs with spruce and fir. Also found along the borders of swamps and lower-elevation forests where conditions are moist and cool; associates there include hobblebush (*Viburnum lantanoides*), goldthread (*Coptis groenlandica*), partridgeberry (*Mitchella repens*), bunchberry (*Cornus canadensis*), and starflower (*Trientalis borealis*).

**Notes:** American mountain-ash is not commercially valuable as a timber species. Its showy clusters of fruit are very sour. Moose browse the twigs and leaves. Fruits are rich in ascorbic acid and Native Americans used them for medicinal purposes. Many birds eat the fruits, including ruffed grouse, catbirds, most thrushes, evening grosbeaks, and pine grosbeaks. The tree occasionally is planted as an ornamental. European mountain-ash, or rowan, is planted widely as an ornamental and may be found in the wild. Compared to American mountain-ash, it grows faster, its fruits are slightly larger (10 to 12 mm across) and orange to orange-yellow, the leaves are rounded or short-pointed at the end, and they are hairy on both sides. The twigs are hairy, the buds are not sticky and are covered with white woolly hair.

---

*In the Field*
- Leaves are odd-pinnately compound, with paired leaflets
- Thirteen to seventeen leaflets, 5 to 8 cm long, with serrated margins, sharply pointed, smooth, light green above and paler below
- Bright orange-red clusters of berry-like fruit
- Most commonly found at high elevation

# EUROPEAN MOUNTAIN-ASH   Sorbier des oiseleurs

Rowan-tree
*Sorbus aucuparia* L.
Rosaceae: Rose Family

**Size and Form.** European mountain-ash is a small tree or shrub, up to 12 m tall, 15 to 38 cm in diameter. The trunk is short with stout, upright branches forming a narrow, oval crown.

**Leaves.** Deciduous, alternate, odd-pinnately compound, 15 to 25 cm long, slender, hairy, with nine to seventeen paired leaflets on short stalks, end leaflet stalked. Leaflets are 3 to 5 cm long,

dull green above, whitish below, and somewhat hairy on both sides, oblong, with serrated margins, blunt or short-pointed. Autumn color: yellow.

**Bark.** Thin, light gray, smooth or somewhat scaly.

**Twigs.** Stout, hairy, grayish brown becoming dark brown.

**Buds.** Terminal bud egg-shaped, 6 to 13 mm long, covered with white, wooly hairs, not sticky, dark purplish red. Lateral buds are similar but smaller, pressed tightly against twig.

**Flowers.** June to July when leaves are fully grown, white, perfect, 8 mm across, borne on short stalks in compact, woolly clusters, 10 to 15 cm across.

**Fruit.** A large berry-like pome, orange to orange-yellow, 10 to 12 mm across, in round-topped clusters. It ripens in autumn and is persistent until spring.

**Distribution.** Native of northern Europe, western Asia, and Siberia. Widely planted as an ornamental in the United States and Canada and naturalized in New England and adjacent Canada.

**Habitat.** Seed spread by birds, found along fencerows, the edges of swamps, and in upland bogs.

**Notes:** Planted as an ornamental because of its showy white flowers and large clusters of orange fruit. The fruits are consumed more readily by birds than those of American mountain-ash.

> ### In the Field
> - Leaves are odd-pinnately compound, with nine to seventeen leaflets oppositely arranged on a slender, hairy rachis
> - Leaflets are somewhat hairy on both sides
> - Terminal bud covered with white, woolly hairs
> - Showy, white clusters of flowers
> - Clusters of orange, berry-like fruit

# SHOWY MOUNTAIN-ASH     Sorbier décoratif

Dogberry, northern mountain-ash
*Sorbus decora* (Sarg.) C.K. Schneid.
Rosaceae: Rose Family

**Size and Form.** Showy mountain-ash is a
small tree or shrub, up to 10 m in height.
The trunk is short with spreading, slender
branches forming a narrow, rounded
crown. Often multiple trunks arise from
root suckers, giving it a shrub-like
appearance.

**Leaves.** Deciduous, alternate,
odd-pinnately compound, 15 to
20 cm long, with thirteen to
seventeen paired leaflets on short
stalks, end leaflet stalked. Leaflets
are blue-green above, paler below,
3 to 8 cm long, blunt-pointed and
narrowly elliptical, with finely
toothed margins from the tip to
middle.

**Bark.** Thin, smooth, with elongated pores, light grayish green
to golden brown, becoming slightly scaly with age.

**Twigs.** Reddish brown to grayish, without hairs.

**Buds.** Terminal buds are pointy and dark reddish brown,
slightly curved, about 10 to 14 cm long, sticky, with hairy inner
scales.

**Flowers.** Late May to early June when leaves are fully-grown,
white, perfect, on short, stout, hairy stalks, in broad, flat, open
clusters.

**Fruit.** A berry-like pome, shiny, red, 8 to 12 mm in diameter, in
many-fruited rounded clusters, ripening in autumn and
persistent until spring.

**Distribution.** Found in northern Maine, New Hampshire, and Vermont, and throughout adjacent Canada. Uncommon in southern Maine, New Hampshire, Vermont, and southern New England.

**Habitat.** Showy mountain-ash is found on thin, rocky soils that may be moist or dry; also along the rocky shores of lakes and rivers.

**Notes:** Showy mountain-ash is a boreal species with a distribution similar to American mountain ash except occurring much farther north in Labrador and Quebec and not as far south in the United States. Showy mountain-ash is not commercially valuable as a timber species. Moose browse the twigs and leaves and its showy clusters of fruit are eaten by some bird species. Endangered in Massachusetts.

> *In the Field*
> • Leaves odd-pinnately compound
> • Leaflets shorter and more blunt-pointed and narrowly elliptic than American mountain-ash, with leaflets lance-shaped and tapering to a point
> • Fruit 8 to 12 mm long, larger than American mountain-ash (up to 6 mm)

# BLACK LOCUST    Robinier faux-acacia

False acacia, locust
*Robinia psuedoacacia* L.
Leguminosae: Legume Family

**Size and Form.** Black locust is a medium-sized tree, up to 18 m tall, 30 to 76 cm in diameter. The trunk may be straight and clear

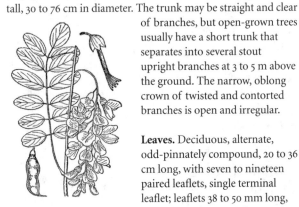

of branches, but open-grown trees usually have a short trunk that separates into several stout upright branches at 3 to 5 m above the ground. The narrow, oblong crown of twisted and contorted branches is open and irregular.

**Leaves.** Deciduous, alternate, odd-pinnately compound, 20 to 36 cm long, with seven to nineteen paired leaflets, single terminal leaflet; leaflets 38 to 50 mm long, 13 to 19 mm wide; elliptical or oval, short, stout petiole; margin smooth; tip notched or bristle-tipped; base rounded; surfaces dull dark blue-green, smooth above; paler and smooth, except for fine hair on the mid-rib, below. Autumn color: yellow.

**Bark.** On mature trees corky, reddish brown to nearly black, deeply furrowed into rounded, interlacing, fibrous, superficially scaly ridges.

**Twigs.** Moderately stout, angular, zigzag, reddish brown, usually with a pair of sharp spines at each leaf scar.

**Buds.** End and lateral buds are tiny, in small clusters, submerged beneath the leaf scar, embedded in the bark. Terminal bud absent.

**Flowers.** May or June after leaves emerge, perfect, fragrant, whitish, pea-like, borne in showy drooping clusters about 14 cm long.

**Fruit.** A many-seeded pod, 7 to 10 cm long, flat, with a thin-walled husk, smooth, dark reddish brown, several on a central stalk; remaining on the tree during winter. Seeds are small, flattish, brown, four to eight per pod.

**Distribution.** In New England and Canada, a naturalized species formerly widely planted as an ornamental, for erosion control, reclamation of deforested sites, or to reforest gravel pits, mine spoils, and similar sites. Native range is the Appalachian Mountains from Pennsylvania southward and in Missouri, Arkansas, and Oklahoma.

**Habitat.** Grows on a wide variety of sites when planted, but does best on moist, well-drained, limestone-derived soils; shade-intolerant. Found along fencerows, roads; rapidly colonizes old fields and disturbed sites. Forms dense clones or thickets through root sprouts. A wide variety of tree species are associated with black locust and eventually replace it.

**Notes:** *Robinia,* dedicated to Jean Robin (1550–1629) and his son Vespasian Robin (1579–1662), herbalists to kings of France and the first to cultivate locust in Europe; and *psuedoacacia,* false acacia, for its resemblance to the true acacia. Black locust is not an important timber species in the region. Major uses include ornamental planting and reclamation of disturbed sites. Nitrogen-fixing bacteria on its roots enrich the soil. Historically, its hard, heavy, strong, very durable wood has been used for railroad ties, mine timbers, insulator pins, ship timbers, tree nails for wooden ship building, pegs, and stakes. Within the region, the wood primarily is used for fence posts because of its extreme durability in contact with the soil and for firewood. Not an important wildlife species but does provide a source of pollen and nectar for honey production.

> ### In the Field
> - Leaves odd-pinnately compound, with seven to nine-teen paired leaflets with terminal leaflet
> - Twigs with thorns in pairs at base of leaf stalks
> - Bark thick, corky, deeply furrowed
> - Flowers showy, white, fragrant, pea-like, in drooping clusters
> - Fruit a pod, flat, about the size of a pea pod, in clusters, containing four to eight small, brown seeds

## AILANTHUS    Ailante glanuleux

Tree-of-heaven
*Ailanthus altissima* (Mill.) Swingle
Simaroubaceae: Quassia Family

**Size and Form.** A medium-sized tree 12 to 18 m tall and 60 to 120 cm in diameter, ailanthus is a coarse, malodorous tree. The

trunk is often crooked and divided, the branches stout, crooked, and wide-spreading, forming an open crown. Short-lived, fast-growing, and shade-intolerant, ailanthus tolerates urban smoke and air pollution.

**Leaves.** Alternate, pinnately compound, 30 to 90 cm long with eleven to forty-one leaflets 5 to 15 cm long, lance-shaped (broadest above the base and tapering toward the tip); margins entire except for two or more coarse gland-tipped teeth on the undersurface at the base; dark green above, paler beneath, smooth, with a disagreeable odor. Petioles smooth, round, swollen at base. Leafs out late in spring and drops leaves quickly after the first hard frost. Autumn colors: yellow or falling without turning color.

**Bark.** Thin, dark or light gray, shallow fissures on old trunks often appear as thin lines.

**Twigs.** Very stout, red-brown to yellow, downy to smooth; leaf scars large with at least nine vein scars in a U-shaped pattern.

**Buds.** Terminal bud absent; lateral buds about 3 mm long, somewhat rounded, brownish, downy.

**Flowers.** June; after the leaves are fully grown; small, yellow-green; borne in upright branching clusters 15 to 30 cm or more long; five greenish hairy petals, male flowers malodorous. Dioecious or perfect flowers borne on the same tree with unisexual flowers.

**Fruit.** Large samara 4 to 5 cm long, twisted, with one seed in the center, reddish or yellow-green turning pale brown when mature, borne in crowded clusters in October.

**Distribution.** Introduced from China, planted and naturalized across much of the North American continent. Formerly widely planted in cities, where it has now become naturalized in waste places. In New England, in eastern Massachusetts, Connecticut, and Rhode Island. Not found in northern New England.

**Habitat.** Ailanthus will grow in almost any upland soil, and frequently is found in extremely dry or disturbed urban sites. Becomes established in warm microsites—near structures, on south-facing slopes, or other protected sites with disturbed soil. Normally does not colonize natural habitats. Root-sprouts form dense, pure stands.

**Notes:** The word *Ailanthus* is from the Indonesian name *ailanthos* (tree of heaven, *A. moluccana*); *altissima* is Latin for "highest" or "tallest." The wood is soft, weak, and open-grained, pale yellow with thick, lighter-colored sapwood and is of no commercial value. Ailanthus was first introduced into the United States from England to Philadelphia, Pennsylvania, in 1784, apparently to provide food for silkworms as in China. A coarse tree that grows and sprouts rapidly, ailanthus roots readily buckle sidewalks and clog drains, and so is not recommended for ornamental planting.

---

### In the Field
- Leaves long, pinnately compound, leaflets with gland-tipped teeth at the base on undersurface, malodorous
- Twigs very stout, smooth, with large leaf scars, malodorous when crushed
- Bark fairly smooth, gray with pale fissure lines, malodorous when cut
- Large clusters of twisted seed cases on female trees
- Dried upright stems of male flowers persist through the following winter
- Occurs on disturbed or urban sites primarily; normally does not colonize natural habitats

# BUTTERNUT   Noyer cendré

White walnut
*Juglans cinerea* L.
Juglandaceae: Walnut Family

**Size and Form.** Butternut is a shade-intolerant, fast-growing tree of eastern North America. A medium-sized tree, 12 to 18 m tall and up to 60 to 100 cm in diameter. The trunk is commonly short on open-grown trees, taller and crooked with few branches when growing in the forest.

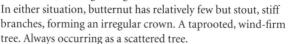

In either situation, butternut has relatively few but stout, stiff branches, forming an irregular crown. A taprooted, wind-firm tree. Always occurring as a scattered tree.

**Leaves.** Alternate, pinnately compound, 40 to 70 cm long; with eleven to seventeen leaflets. Leaflets 8 to 10 cm long and half as wide, sticky when young, progressively larger toward the tip, pointed oval with fine teeth, yellow-green, rough, densely hairy on lower surfaces. Leaflets sessile except the terminal one, which usually is present and which readily distinguishes it from black walnut. Autumn color: yellow.

**Bark.** Light gray, fairly smooth on young trees, becoming ridged and grooved with narrow, shallow fissures and wide, irregular, flattened grooves with intersecting ridges.

**Twigs.** Stout, hairy, orange-yellow or rusty brown, sometimes bright green, older twigs becoming smooth and light gray. Leaf scars conspicuous, upper margin straight, usually bordered by a downy pad or "moustache," and containing three U-shaped groups of vein scars. Pith dark brown, chambered (compare to black walnut, page 187).

**Buds.** Terminal bud 12 to 18 mm long, oblong, fairly blunt-tipped, somewhat flattened, pale yellow to light brown, hairy. Lateral buds small, round, pubescent, hairy, located above the leaf scar.

**Flowers.** May (early June in northern New England), with the leaves, monoecious. Male flowers in catkins 6 to 14 cm long borne on a hairy bract; female flowers solitary or in erect clusters on a common stalk, about 8 mm long, with sticky bracts, bright red.

**Fruit.** An oblong-oval nut, 3.8 to 5.5 cm long, four-ridged, sculptured, pointed, covered by a fleshy, green, sticky-downy husk , ripening in autumn, singly or in clusters of three to five; nut shell contains a sweet, oily, edible kernel.

**Distribution.** In New England, widespread except absent from eastern Massachusetts, northeastern Vermont, northern New Hampshire, and northern Maine. In Maritime Canada, restricted to southern and central New Brunswick. Elsewhere, the native range extends south to northernmost Georgia and Arkansas, westward to Minnesota, and southernmost Ontario and Quebec. The range of butternut and black walnut overlap, but butternut occurs farther north and not as far south as black walnut.

**Habitat.** Characteristic of moist, fertile, rocky soils of lower slopes and coves, but also grows on dry, rocky soils. Normally occurs singly in mesic hardwood forests. Associated trees commonly include sugar maple, red maple, red oak, American elm, eastern hemlock, and white pine. On dry sites, redcedar and white pine are common associated trees.

**Notes:** The word *Juglans* means "Jupiter's nut," the classical Latin name for the walnut tree, and *cinerea* means "ash colored." Butternut is not an important timber tree because of its scattered distribution in mixed hardwood stands. The wood is chestnut brown with red tinges, similar to black walnut, but lighter in color and weight. Uses include lumber, furniture, mill work, veneer, carving, and woodenware. Butternut is more prized for its sweet nuts than for its wood. The nut kernels are larger, sweeter, and more easily extracted than those of black walnuts. Butternut is not used as an ornamental; the tree leafs out late in spring and sheds leaves early in fall, and does not transplant well because of its deep taproot. The nuts are eaten and disseminated by squirrels; unrecovered buried nuts facilitate reproduction. Butternut often is attacked by butternut canker (*Sirococcus elavignenti-juglandacearum*), which is fatal to the tree.

### In the Field

- Pinnately compound leaves, leaves very hairy beneath, rachis sticky, hairy
- Terminal leaflet (normally present) as large as the paired adjacent leaflets
- Leaf scar is flat on the upper edge with an adjacent pad ("moustache") of hairs
- Fruit shaped somewhat like a lemon, sticky and downy (compare to black walnut, page 187)
- Pith dark brown, chambered (compare to black walnut, page 187)

# BLACK WALNUT    Noyer noir

American walnut
*Juglans nigra* L.
Juglandaceae: Walnut Family

**Size and Form.** Black walnut is a large tree, 20 to 30 m tall and 60 to 120 cm in diameter; open-grown trees develop massive short trunks, heavy branches, and spreading, open crowns; forest trees have straight trunks with little taper and small rounded, crowns.

**Leaves.** Alternate, large pinnately compound, 30 to 60 cm long; with thirteen to twenty-three short-stalked, lance-shaped leaflets 5 to 10 cm long; terminal leaflet often missing or much smaller than adjacent leaflets; with tapering points and sharply toothed margins; thin, yellow-green above, softly hairy beneath; rachis stout, softly hairy. Foliage aromatic when crushed. Autumn color: yellowish green.

**Bark.** On young trees, light brown and scaly, becoming thick, dark brown-black, and deeply furrowed by broad, rounded, intersecting ridges.

**Twigs.** Stout, brown or orange-brown, and somewhat hairy. Leaf scars conspicuous, V-shaped on upper margin. Pith light brown, chambered.

**Buds.** Terminal bud oval, stout, pale gray, slightly flattened, 6 to 8 mm long and about as wide, blunt-tipped, sparsely covered with silky hairs; lateral buds much smaller.

**Flowers.** May, with the leaves, monoecious. Male flowers in light green, drooping catkins 8 to 12 cm long, female flowers in erect clusters of one to four on a common stalk, about 6 mm long.

**Fruit.** A round or oblong hard nut 3 to 4 cm in diameter, deeply sculptured, covered with a thick, yellowish green husk that is covered with clusters of hairs, not sticky; ripening in autumn, borne singly or in clusters of two to four. Husk distinctively aromatic. Shell contains a sweet, edible, oily kernel.

**Distribution.** Uncommon in New England and adjacent Canada, black walnut is distributed widely in the eastern United States. Its natural range extends from western Vermont, western Massachusetts, and northwestern Connecticut west through New York and southern Ontario to eastern South Dakota, south central Texas; excluding the Mississippi River Valley and Delta, it ranges east to northwestern Florida and Georgia.

**Habitat.** Though widespread, black walnut is very sensitive to soil moisture and fertility. It grows best on warm, deep, fertile, moist, well-drained alluvial soils. In eastern forests, black walnut commonly is found with white ash, sugar maple, black cherry, American beech, basswood, and red oak—species that also do best on deep, fertile, moist well-drained soils. In the Midwest it commonly is planted in groves for future timber or nut harvest. Black walnut is shade-intolerant and fairly fast-growing.

**Notes:** The word *Juglans* means "Jupiter's nut," the classical Latin name for the walnut tree, and *nigra* is Latin for black. Black walnut is valued for its wood, which is easily worked and finished, and is dimensionally stable. It is one of the most valuable timber trees, per board-foot, in eastern North America, widely planted for wood and nuts. Young trees have taproots and are difficult to transplant. It is heavy, hard, strong, rich dark brown with cream-colored sapwood. It is used for fine furniture, veneer, cabinetry, gunstocks, caskets, and woodenware. Walnut roots exude a chemical, juglone, which inhibits the growth of most other plants under or near a walnut tree, therefore it is not a commonly planted lawn tree. Squirrels and other rodents bury the nuts; unrecovered ones facilitate reproduction. When harvesting nuts, the hands become deeply stained yellow by the husks. Crushed walnut shell is used in polishing metal. The foliage is a major food of the luna moth caterpillar (*Actias luna*).

> **In the Field**
> - Pinnately compound leaves with short-stalked leaflets; terminal leaflet often missing, rachis fairly stout, softly hairy
> - Upper margin of leaf scar is V-shaped, and lacks a hairy pad or "moustache"
> - The nut is round with an aromatic husk and not sticky (compare to butternut, page 184)
> - Pith light brown, chambered (compare to butternut, page 184)

# BITTERNUT HICKORY     Caryer cordiforme

Swamp hickory
*Carya cordiformis* (Wangenheim) K. Koch
Juglandaceae: Walnut Family

**Size and Form.** Bitternut hickory is a
medium to large-sized tree up to 25 m tall
and 50 cm in diameter. The trunk is
normally straight with little taper; forest-
grown trees have branch-free boles for a
considerable height and rounded crowns
with short ascending branches; open-

grown specimens have short, sometimes forked trunks and
wide-spread crowns. Bitternut hickory is not a true hickory; it
belongs to the subgenus *Apocarya*, the pecan-hickories. True
hickories sprout when cut, unlike pecan-hickories.

**Leaves.** Alternate, pinnately compound, 12 to 25 cm long; with
seven to eleven stalkless, slender leaflets, the terminal one 10 to
15 cm long and about one-quarter as wide; lance-shaped, long-
pointed, finely toothed; the terminal leaflet is seldom larger
than the uppermost pair; shiny, bright green above, paler with
somewhat hairy veins beneath.
Leaves fragrant when crushed.
Rachis slender and hairy. Autumn
color: bright golden yellow.

**Bark.** On young trees, greenish
gray with irregular yellow or
yellow-orange vertical lines,
remaining smooth for many years.
With age, gradually separates into
shallow, narrow fissures and
intersecting ridges—always tight,
never with loose plates or scales.

**Twigs.** Slender, smooth, minutely hairy so appearing shiny,
greenish to grayish brown, eventually becoming gray.

**Buds.** Terminal bud 1.2 to 2 cm long, slender, long-pointed,
flattened, with two to four scales that meet but do not overlap,

deep yellow, granular. Lateral buds smaller, usually forming singly, sometimes more, immediately above a leaf scar.

**Flowers.** May to June, with the leaves, monoecious. Male flowers in catkins in clusters of three, 8 to 10 cm long, on a common stalk 2 to 3 cm long. Female flowers in two- to five-flowered, short, greenish, hairy spikes.

**Fruit.** A nut, enclosed in a thin, spherical husk, broadest toward the tip, 20 to 35 mm long, solitary or in pairs. The husk is covered with matted yellow hairs, with four ridges descending below a short tip. Nut flattened, widest near the base, with a thin shell. Kernel reddish brown, bitter, inedible.

**Distribution.** Throughout southern and central parts of New England, including west-central Vermont and the Connecticut River Valley; absent from Cape Cod, Maine, and northeastern Vermont and most of New Hampshire. In Canada, occurs in southern Ontario and southern Quebec. Bitternut hickory is the most abundant and widespread hickory in Canada. Elsewhere, bitternut is one of the most abundant and most uniformly distributed of all the hickories, occurring throughout the eastern United States.

**Habitat.** Bitternut hickory occurs on moist lowlands and rich upland soils; it is characteristic of low-lying mesic hardwood forests on deep, moist, fertile soils; also occurs on stream banks and in mountain valleys. It always occurs with other broadleaved trees, including red oak, sugar maple, basswood, white ash, shagbark hickory, black ash, and silver maple.

**Notes:** The word *Carya* is from the Greek *Karua* for walnut tree. The wood is heavy, hard, strong, and tough, but not to the extent of the true hickories; shagbark, pignut, and mockernut. Uses are similar to the true hickories. Bitternut hickory is moderately shade-tolerant, especially as a seedling, moderately slow-growing, shorter-lived than true hickories. Wild turkeys and other wildlife species eat the nuts.

### In the Field
- Leaves pinnately compound, usually with seven or nine narrow leaflets
- Buds bright yellow, covered with small rough scales, appearing naked
- Husk four-ridged below sharp tip; shell thin, can be cut with a knife
- Bark tight, smooth or with narrow interlacing ridges, not shaggy
- Found in fertile, cool, moist hardwood forests

# PIGNUT HICKORY   Carrya glabra

Red hickory, false shagbark hickory
*Carya glabra* (Miller) Sweet
Juglandaceae: Walnut Family

**Size and Form.** Pignut hickory is a small to
medium-sized tree, 15 to 20 m tall and 30 to
80 cm in diameter. In the forest, it develops
an irregular, narrow, open crown of slender,
crooked branches, but open-grown
specimens develop a symmetrical oblong
crown.

**Leaves.** Alternate, pinnately compound, 20 to 30 cm long; with
five to seven (normally five, rarely nine) leaflets, the terminal

one 8 to 15 cm long, 5 to 6 cm
wide, the others nearly stalkless;
lance-shaped with narrow,
pointed tips, finely toothed,
mature leaflets not fringed with
hair, thick, shiny, dark yellow-
green above, paler beneath, fine
hairs on large veins and mid-rib.
Rachis long and slender, foliage
fragrant when crushed. Autumn
color: yellow-brown.

**Bark.** Thin, gray, smooth, and hard with narrow fissures on
young trees, becoming scaly—not shaggy—with narrow
intersecting ridges with age.

**Twigs.** Slender, smooth, greenish, shiny, sometimes with long
ridges, becoming red-gray and finally gray.

**Buds.** Terminal bud small, 6 to 9 mm long, variable in shape
but typically ovoid, greenish gray, somewhat pointed; outer
scales shed in early autumn exposing the small stout, hairy bud.
Lateral buds smaller, broad, blunt-tipped.

**Flowers.** May to June, with the leaves, monoecious. Male
flowers in clusters of three hanging slender catkins, 8 to 18 cm

long, yellow-green with orange anthers. Female flowers in crowded two- to five-flowered spikes, 6 mm long, yellow, the surrounding bracts four-toothed, hairy.

**Fruit.** A nut, enclosed in a pear-shaped thin husk, 25 to 50 mm long. Husk variously splits at the top, or along one or more sutures to the base; nut somewhat flattened, four-ribbed or not, shell thin or thick, enclosing a nut containing a kernel that is difficult to remove and very variable in flavor, sweet or bitter.

**Distribution.** In New England throughout Connecticut, Rhode Island, and Massachusetts, except the northern Berkshire Hills; also southern Vermont and New Hampshire. Rare in Canada— only scattered locations in southernmost Ontario. Elsewhere from eastern New York west to southern Michigan, south to Louisiana, east to central Florida. Absent from the lower Mississippi River Valley.

**Habitat.** Strictly an upland species, occurring on dry to dry-mesic well-drained soils. Common but not abundant on ridgetops and side slopes throughout the oak-hickory forest, where it is usually found with red, black, and white oaks, white ash, shagbark hickory, black cherry, and hop hornbeam. Generally not found with sugar maple or basswood on mesic sites.

**Notes:** The word *glabra* is Latin for "smooth," referring to the bark. Pignut hickory is slow-growing and long-lived, fairly shade-tolerant as a seedling. It sprouts profusely after fire or cutting. The wood is hard, heavy, very strong, and dark brown; uses the same as shagbark hickory and sold as hickory. The nuts are an important wildlife food for a wide range of species including squirrels, chipmunks, deer, bear, foxes, raccoon, and wild turkeys. Deer also browse the leaves and twigs.

**In the Field**
- Leaves pinnately compound, usually five leaflets
- Bark tight with shallow fissures, not shaggy
- Twigs slender, normally hairless
- Fruit pear-shaped with a thin husk
- Terminal bud small, downy, onion-shaped
- Typical of dry oak-hickory forests

# SHAGBARK HICKORY    Caryer ovale

Upland hickory
*Carya ovata* (Mill) K. Koch
Juglandaceae: Walnut Family

**Size and Form.** Shagbark hickory is a
medium-sized to large tree, up to 25 m
tall, 60 cm in diameter, and can live to be
200 years old. The trunk is normally
straight, relatively slender for its height,
with little taper. In the forest, the trunk is
often branch-free for up to three-quarters
of its length. The crown is fairly open, with a few stout,
ascending limbs and branches.

**Leaves.** Alternate, pinnately compound, 20 to 25 cm long, with
five, rarely seven, leaflets; all leaflets widest at the middle, the
terminal leaflet 13 to 18 cm long, larger than the laterals, pointed

at both ends, and finely toothed
with two or three tufts of hair per
tooth; thick, firm, hairless,
yellowish green above, paler
beneath. Fragrant when crushed.
Rachis stout, sometimes hairy,
slightly grooved. Autumn color:
golden yellow.

**Bark.** Thin, smooth, and gray on
young trunks; with age becoming
dark gray and separating in thin, narrow plates 30 or more cm
long, free at the lower end or at both ends, that curve outward,
giving a characteristic shaggy look.

**Twigs.** Stout, shiny, reddish brown, to gray-brown, becoming
gray.

**Buds.** Terminal bud egg-shaped, 12 to 18 mm long, blunt-
pointed, greenish brown or brown, with four to six overlapping
scales, the outer ones commonly spreading and sometimes
broken, the inner ones densely hairy. Lateral buds smaller,
divergent from twig.

**Flowers.** May to June, with the leaves, monoecious. Male flowers in catkins in clusters of three, 10 to 13 cm long, yellow-green, on a common stalk 2 to 3 cm long. Female flowers in small clusters enclosed by (usually) four fused bracts with free tips, yellow, sparsely hairy.

**Fruit.** Nut encased in a thick, woody spherical husk, 3 to 5 cm long, wider than long, splitting to the base in four sections when fruit is ripe; solitary or in pairs. Shell of nut thin, hard, containing a sweet, edible kernel.

**Distribution.** In New England throughout Connecticut, Rhode Island, and Massachusetts; rare in Plymouth County and Cape Cod, also occurs in southern and western Vermont, southern New Hampshire, and Down East Maine. In Canada, occurs from southern Ontario along the St. Lawrence River into southern Quebec. Elsewhere, found throughout most of the eastern United States from New York (except the Adirondack Mountains) west to Wisconsin, south to Louisiana.

**Habitat.** Grows best in humid climates and on rich, moist soils of hillsides and in valleys. Shagbark is the hardiest of the hickories, however, and occurs on a wide variety of sites; in New England, associated with sugar maple, beech, and red oak. In the North most commonly found on south-facing slopes. Also occurs on dry sites and drier parts of river floodplains, but does not tolerate prolonged soil saturation.

**Notes:** The word *ovata* is Latin for "egg-shaped," referring (poorly) to the shape of the nut. Fairly shade-tolerant as a seedling, existing in the understory for many years until a canopy disturbance makes a gap for it to reach the overstory. Slow-growing, long-lived, and quite free of disease and insect pests. The most distinctive of the hickories found growing in the region because of its shaggy bark. Shagbark and pignut hickories supply most of the wood sold as hickory. The wood is heavy, very hard, strong, and shock resistant but difficult to season. Uses include tool handles, ladder rungs, furniture, cabinetry, flooring, and veneer. Primary source of edible hickory nuts; wood used to cure meats, make charcoal, and provide excellent firewood. Wild turkeys, bears, squirrels, and chipmunks consume the nuts.

### In the Field

- Leaves pinnately compound with five leaflets, center leaflet largest, all fringed with minute tufts of hair
- Bark in long plates, free at one or both ends and curving outward, making the trunk appear shaggy
- Twigs smooth, with small, dark orange pores
- Terminal bud large, with somewhat loose, spreading scales
- Fruit with thick husk, splitting freely to the base and separating completely; the nut itself light yellow brown, wider than long, kernel sweet, edible

# MOCKERNUT HICKORY

White hickory
*Carya alba* (L.) Nutt. [*Carya tomentosa*]
Juglandaceae: Walnut Family

**Size and Form.** Common in southern New
England, mockernut hickory is a large tree,
up to 30 m tall and 90 cm in diameter.
Unlike the other New England hickories, it
develops a large, dense crown. It is the most
abundant hickory in the eastern United
States.

**Leaves.** Alternate, pinnately compound, 20 to 35 cm long; with
seven or nine (occasionally five) leaflets, leaflets 5 to 7 cm long;
margins toothed, oblong lance-shaped, pointed at the tip,
rounded at the base; smooth, dark yellow-green above, paler

beneath and hairy; very fragrant
when crushed. Rachis stout, hairy,
flattened, and grooved. Autumn
color: yellow or russet.

**Bark.** Gray, tight with low ridges
and shallow fissures, not
separating into plates.

**Twigs.** Stout, reddish brown or
gray, pith solid.

**Buds.** Reddish brown, somewhat globe-shaped, tomentose,
bud scales overlapping like roof shingles; terminal 8.5 to 19 mm
long, laterals smaller.

**Flowers.** May to early June, when leaves are about half-grown,
monoecious. Male flowers in catkins in clusters of three, 10 to
13 cm long at axils of leaves of previous season or from inner
scales of the terminal bud at the base of current growth.
Female flowers in short spikes on stalks that terminate in shoots
of the current year. Male flowers generally emerge before the
female flowers.

**Fruit.** A nut in a thick, four-ribbed, dark reddish brown husk, solitary or paired; oblong or oval-shaped, ripening in September and October, 3.8 to 5 cm long. Nut with a short, neck-like base, four-ridged, with a pale reddish brown, very thick shell containing a small, dark brown, sweet, edible kernel. Mockernut hickory produces one of the heaviest seeds among hickories. Squirrels are the primary dispersers, often burying seed substantial distances from the tree.

**Distribution.** In New England, mockernut hickory occurs in eastern Massachusetts, including Cape Cod, the Connecticut River Valley, as well as southern Connecticut and Rhode Island. Elsewhere it occurs from southeastern New York, southern Pennsylvania, Ohio, and Indiana west to Missouri, south to east Texas, and east to central Florida. Absent from the lower Mississippi River Valley.

**Habitat.** In New England, mockernut hickory is found on dry, but fertile upland soils and hillsides, especially fine sandy soils that were once plowed or pastured. It is found singly or in small groups associated with oak-hickory and beech-maple forests, frequently found with scarlet, red, and white oaks, pignut and shagbark hickories.

**Notes:** The word *alba* is Latin for "white." Mockernuts are consumed readily by several species of wildlife, especially gray squirrels, which eat the green nuts. Black bears, foxes, white-footed mice, and wild turkeys also feed on the fallen ripe nuts. White-tailed deer browse the twigs and foliage and feed on the nuts. The wood is hard, heavy, very strong and dark brown; uses the same as shagbark hickory and sold as hickory. Mockernut is the preferred wood for smoking hams.

> ### In the Field
> - Leaves alternate, pinnately compound, with seven or nine leaflets; rachis stout, hairy
> - Bark gray, tight, with low ridges and shallow fissures
> - Buds with overlapping scales, like shingles on a roof
> - Fruit has thick, four-part husk that splits from the middle to the base, nut shell red-brown, very hard

## BOXELDER    Érable à feuilles composées

Ash-leaf maple, Manitoba maple
*Acer negundo* L.
Aceraceae: Maple Family

**Size and Form.** Small to medium-sized tree,
15 to 23 m tall and 30 to 80 cm in diameter.
Trunk commonly divided into several stout,
diverging branches forming a broad, open,
asymmetrical crown. Unique among native
maples in that it has compound leaves,
resembling ash.

**Leaves.** Opposite, 15 to 38 cm
long, pinnately compound with
three to five leaflets (rarely seven
to nine), leaflets 5 to 12 cm long,
variable in shape, asymmetrically
toothed, upper surface light
green, gray-green beneath, veins
prominent. Rachis slender,
enlarged at base. Autumn color:
yellow.

**Bark.** On young trees smooth, light gray-brown; becoming
deeply furrowed into narrow ridges and more brown with age.

**Twigs.** Stout or moderately so, green or greenish purple to
brown, shiny with a waxy bloom that is easily rubbed off.
Prominent leaf scars V-shaped, opposite scars meet around the
twig.

**Buds.** Terminal bud 3 to 8 mm long, rather blunt, with two to
four red-brown scales with fine white hairs; lateral buds almost

as large, pressed against twig, within the leaf base so not visible until the leaf falls off.

**Flowers.** April to May, just before or with the leaves; small with pale yellow-green sepals, no petals, male flowers in clusters on long, thin, hairy pedicels, female flowers in drooping clusters, borne near the base of new twigs; dioecious.

**Fruit.** Paired samaras; wings 3 to 4 cm long, incurved, seed case narrow, pointed, and wrinkled. Born in drooping clusters, maturing in autumn, often remaining on the tree over winter.

**Distribution.** The most widely distributed of all North American maples, boxelder occurs from coast to coast and from Canada to Guatemala, although distribution is scattered in the far western United States. The primary contiguous range is from New York to central Florida and west to southern Texas and eastern Alberta, central Saskatchewan, and Manitoba. Native range in New England was scattered but it has become naturalized locally in much of New England.

**Habitat.** In much of its range, boxelder grows on lakeshores and along streams, even on sites that are seasonally flooded. In New England and elsewhere, it colonizes roadsides and disturbed open sites. Intolerant of shade, survives on most soils, and highly resistant to drought and frost. In its natural range, boxelder commonly is associated with river floodplain and bottomland species that occur on moist, alluvial soils: cottonwood, black willow, sycamore, silver maple, and red ash.

**Notes:** Because of its ease of transplanting, rapid growth, and resistance to drought, boxelder once was planted widely as a street and yard tree and as a shelterbelt tree on the Great Plains. It is fast-growing, short-lived, and sprouts readily after injury. Of little importance as a timber species, the wood is similar to red and silver maples and when cut is sold as soft maple. The seeds are consumed by a wide variety of birds and mammals; because of the persistent fruiting habit, seeds are available throughout the winter, making boxelder an especially valuable wildlife food source.

### In the Field

- Leaves opposite, pinnately compound with three to five leaflets (rarely more), leaflets 5 to 12 cm long, variable in shape, asymmetrically toothed, upper surface light green
- Terminal bud 3 to 8 mm long, rather blunt, with two to four red-brown scales with fine white hairs
- Twigs bright green (purple in winter) with a waxy bloom that is easily rubbed off
- Fruit maturing in autumn; 3 to 4 cm long, incurved, seed case narrow, pointed, and wrinkled
- Samaras borne in abundant drooping clusters, often remaining on the tree over winter

# WHITE ASH    Frêne blanc

Biltmore ash, Biltmore white ash
*Fraxinus americana* L.
Oleaceae: Olive Family

**Size and Form.** White ash is a medium-sized to large tree, up to 30 m high, 60 to 90 cm in diameter. In the forest, the trunk is long, massive, straight, free of branches, with a narrow, pyramidal crown. In the open, the crown is broadly pyramidal or oblong and round-topped, with branches extending almost to the ground.

**Leaves.** Deciduous, opposite, pinnately compound, 20 to 38 cm long, hairless, stout, grooved. There are an odd number of leaflets, five to nine (usually seven), 7 to 13 cm long, about half as wide, oval to lance-shaped, margins smooth or with

infrequent rounded teeth; dark green and hairless above, much paler below, hairless except along the veins, on short stalks. Autumn color: deep red to purple.

**Bark.** On young trees, bark is light gray, smooth, with an orange tinge. Bark on older trees is thick, light gray, finely furrowed into narrow interlacing ridges in a regular diamond pattern.

**Twigs.** Stout, hairless, dark green to grayish or brownish green, shiny, with conspicuous pale pores. The outer layer of the twigs flakes or peels, forming a loose, waxy covering on all but new shoots. The upper margins of the leaf scars have a V- or U-shaped notch.

**Buds.** Terminal bud is 5 to 14 mm long, broadly egg-shaped, blunt, covered with four to six dark brown scales. Lateral buds are smaller, blunter, uppermost laterals buds adjacent to the terminal bud.

**Flowers.** May, with or just ahead of the leaves, dioecious. Male flowers borne in purple clusters; female flowers are minute and in clusters.

**Fruit.** A winged seed, 2.5 to 5 cm long, in drooping clusters, persistent until midwinter and into the following spring. Wing covers only the tip of the seed case.

**Distribution.** Occurs throughout New England and adjacent Canada. Grows naturally from Cape Breton Island, Nova Scotia, west to Minnesota and south to Texas and Florida; the most abundant native ash.

**Habitat.** White ash occurs on rich, deep, moderately well-drained upland soils in mixtures with other hardwoods and occasionally softwoods. It is never a dominant species in the forest. Associates include eastern white pine, northern red oak, white oak, sugar maple, red maple, yellow birch, American beech, black cherry, American basswood, and eastern hemlock. Small trees and shrubs associated with ash include downy serviceberry, American hornbeam, witch-hazel (*Hamamelis virginiana* L.), flowering dogwood, eastern hop hornbeam, and maple-leaved viburnum (*Viburnum acerifolium* L.).

**Notes:** White ash is a valuable timber species, accounting for most of the ash lumber produced. The heartwood is light brown or grayish brown; the creamy white sapwood may be very wide. Because white ash wood is hard, tough, strong, and highly resistant to shock, it is desirable for tool handles, oars and paddles, snowshoes, baseball bats, and other sporting goods. It also is used in unupholstered furniture, flooring, and millwork. It is planted as an ornamental. White ash seed is a food source for birds such as cardinals, purple finches, evening grosbeaks, and pine grosbeaks, as well as small mammals. Moose and white-tailed deer browse the young shoots. White ash is subject to periodic decline thought to be caused by drought, winter injuries, or water table fluctuations, resulting in dieback and mortality. Ash yellows, commonly associated with decline, is caused by a bacteria-like organism. More recently the emerald ash borer (*Agrilus planipennis*), an invasive pest from Asia, has caused serious mortality in ash in the midwestern United States and Ontario.

### In the Field

- Opposite, pinnately compound leaves, usually with seven leaflets, with smooth margins or few, rounded teeth
- Twigs stout and hairless, upper margin of leaf scar with a V- or U-shaped notch
- Uppermost lateral buds adjacent to the terminal bud
- Fruit wing enclosing only the tip of the seed case
- Leaves turn deep red to purple in autum

# BLACK ASH    Frêne noir

Basket ash, brown ash, swamp ash
*Fraxinus nigra* Marsh.
Oleaceae: Olive Family

**Size and Form.** Black ash is a small to medium-sized tree, up to 21 m high, 30 to 60 cm in diameter. The trunk is slender, often leaning or crooked, with a narrow, open crown of coarse, upright branches. In the open, the tree is shorter with a broader and round-topped crown.

**Leaves.** Leaves are deciduous, opposite, pinnately compound, 30 to 40 cm long; stout, hairless, grooved. There is an odd

number of leaflets, seven to eleven, 10 to 13 cm long, about a quarter as wide, oblong, tapering to a long, pointed tip, margin finely and sharply toothed; dark green and hairless above, paler below, hairless except for tufts of hair where the leaflets attach to the main leaf stem; leaflets are without stalks. Autumn color: yellow and brown.

**Bark.** Bark is thin, soft, ashy gray, and scaly, with corky ridges that easily rub off.

**Twigs.** Twigs are stout, hairless, dark green with conspicuous raised pores, becoming dark gray.

**Buds.** Terminal bud is 6 to 10 mm long, egg-shaped, pointed, dark brown to nearly black, covered by four to six scales. Lateral buds are smaller, uppermost pair of buds set down below the terminal.

**Flowers.** May, with or just ahead of the leaves. Flowers perfect or unisexual on the same tree or separate trees. Male and female flowers borne in clusters.

**Fruit.** A winged seed, 2.5 to 4.5 cm long, in drooping clusters, persistent until midwinter and into the following spring. Wing covers the entire seed case.

**Distribution.** Occurs throughout New England and adjacent Canada except for the New Hampshire seacoast, eastern Massachusetts, Rhode Island, and eastern Connecticut. Native range extends from Newfoundland and Cape Breton Island, Nova Scotia, west to southeastern Manitoba, and south to Iowa, West Virginia, and New Jersey.

**Habitat.** Black ash is a slow-growing tree characteristic of cool, poorly drained sites and organic soils, such as swamps, bogs, bottomlands, and along sluggish rivers. Associates include red maple, American elm, northern white-cedar, balsam fir, black spruce, eastern hemlock, yellow birch, tamarack, and speckled alder (*Alnus incana* (L.) Moench subsp. *rugosa* (Du Roi) Clausen).

**Notes:** Wood similar but inferior to that of white ash, included with white ash in the trade. Special uses of black ash wood are due to its flexibility and that it can be made to separate along the annual rings by pounding. It was a preferred wood for snowshoes, barrel hoops, and canoe ribs. Native Americans have long used strips of black ash for basket weaving and that use has continued. Seeds are a source of food for song and game birds and small mammals; they are reported to be an important source of food for wood ducks. Moose and white-tailed deer browse the twigs and leaves.

> ### In the Field
> - Opposite, pinnately compound leaves, with seven to eleven leaflets, margins with fine, sharp teeth; without stalks
> - Uppermost pair of lateral buds set distinctly below the terminal bud
> - Seed wing covers the entire seed
> - Bark with soft corky ridges that can be easily rubbed off
> - Occurs on cool, poorly drained sites

# RED ASH   Frêne rouge

Green ash, water ash, swamp ash
*Fraxinus pennsylvanica* Marsh.
Oleaceae: Olive Family

**Size and Form.** Red ash is a small to
medium-sized tree, up to 18 m tall, 30 to 60
cm in diameter. Variable in form, the trunk
may be straight with a rounded crown,
stout, leaning, or slender; or crooked and
shrub-like.

**Leaves.** Deciduous, opposite, pinnately compound, 15 to 24
cm long; rachis stout, grooved, hairy. There are an odd
number of leaflets, five to nine (usually seven), 8 to 13 cm
long, about a third as wide, oval, tapering to a point, margin
toothed above the middle; pale yellowish green and hairless
above, slightly paler below,
densely hairy, on short, stout,
hairy petioles. Autumn color:
yellow.

**Bark.** On young trees bark is light
gray, smooth, with a red tinge.
Bark on mature trees is thick,
grayish brown, with many
vertical, shallow furrows and
interlacing ridges in an irregular
diamond pattern.

**Twigs.** Moderately stout, flattened at the nodes, ashy gray to
pale reddish brown, generally densely hairy.

**Buds.** Terminal bud is 3 to 8 mm long, rounded, reddish
brown, and hairy. Lateral buds are smaller, uppermost buds
very close to the terminal but not adjacent as in white ash.

**Flowers.** Appear in May, with or just ahead of the leaves,
dioecious. Male and female flowers borne in clusters, on hairy
stems.

**Fruit.** A winged seed, 2.5 to 5 cm long, in drooping clusters, persistent until midwinter and into the following spring. Wing covers a half or more of the seed case.

**Distribution.** Occurs throughout southern New England, eastern Maine, southeastern New Hampshire, Champlain Valley in Vermont, most of New Brunswick, and adjacent southeastern Quebec. It is the most widely distributed ash in the United States and Canada, extending from Cape Breton Island, Nova Scotia, west to southeastern Alberta and south through Wyoming to southeastern Texas and northern Florida and Georgia.

**Habitat.** Found on poorly drained or seasonally flooded sites, stream or lakeshores, bottomlands, and floodplains. Also found on disturbed sites with seasonally high water tables, such as roadside ditches and old fields. Associates include boxelder, red maple, American sycamore, eastern cottonwood, quaking aspen, black willow, and American elm.

**Notes:** Wood similar but inferior to that of white ash, included with white ash in the trade. Uses are the same as white ash. Planted as an ornamental, and in reclamation of mine spoil banks. Seeds are eaten by a number of birds and mammals, including wood ducks, evening grosbeaks, pine grosbeaks, and white-footed mice.

> ### In the Field
> - Leaf undersurface and stalks densely hairy, margins with teeth above the middle
> - Uppermost lateral buds very close to the terminal but not adjacent as in white ash (page 204)
> - Twigs usually densely hairy, twigs lacking hair do not exhibit flaking or peeling of the surface (as with white ash, page 204)
> - Wing covers a half or more of the seed case

## HONEY LOCUST  Févier épineux

Thorny-locust, sweet-locust
*Gleditsia triacanthos* L.
Leguminosae: Legume Family

**Size and Form.** Honey locust is a medium-sized tree, up to 24 m tall, 30 to 60 cm in diameter, the trunk is short; crown is open, broad, flat-topped.

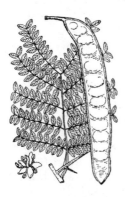

**Leaves.** Alternate and both pinnately and doubly pinnately compound. Pinnately compound leaves with eighteen to twenty-eight leaflets, no terminal leaflet, 2.5 to 5 cm long, oval to elliptical; margin with fine, rounded teeth; smooth, dark green, shiny above; dull yellow-green, smooth or nearly so below. Doubly pinnate leaves with four to seven pairs of pinnae, about 16 cm long; leaflets similar to pinnately compound leaves but smaller; rachis grooved above, hairy, swollen, at the base. Autumn color: yellow.

**Bark.** Mature bark grayish brown to nearly black, usually roughened and broken up into long, narrow, longitudinal and superficially scaly ridges, separated by deep fissures; often with numerous clusters of large, many-branched thorns.

**Twigs.** Stout to slender, zigzag, greenish to reddish brown, shiny, with single and branched thorns 7.6 to 10 cm long.

**Buds.** Terminal bud absent, twig ends in a withered stub. Lateral buds are tiny, in vertical rows, submerged beneath the leaf scar, embedded in the bark.

**Flowers.** June when the leaves are almost fully grown, polygamous. Flowers are greenish white, small, about 5 mm across. Male flowers in many-flowered drooping clusters, 5 to 7 cm long. Female flowers in few-flowered drooping clusters, 7 to 9 cm long.

**Fruit.** A many-seeded pod, 15 to 40 cm long, flat, curved and twisted, tapering at both ends, brownish, falling in fall and winter without opening. Seeds are bean-like, brown, about 7 mm long, twelve to fourteen per pod, in a sweet pulp.

**Distribution.** Honey locust is a tree of the southeastern and midwestern United States. It is planted as an ornamental and hedge plant and naturalized in our region. Grows on a wide variety of sites when planted, but does best on deep, moist, limestone-derived soils, shade-intolerant.

**Notes:** The genus name *Gleditsia* honors Johann Gottleib Gleditsch (1714–1786), director of the Berlin Botanic Garden; *triacanthos,* "with three spines," referring to the familiar form of the branched thorns. Honey locust is not an important timber species in our region. Major use is for ornamental planting. Cultivars used in ornamental planting have neither thorns nor fruit. Its wood is hard, heavy, strong, cross-grained, and resistant to decay; it has been used for railroad ties and fence posts. In the region, the wood primarily is used for fence posts because of its durability in contact with the soil. Seed pods are a source of food for mammals and birds.

---

### In the Field
- Leaves singly and doubly pinnately compound
- Bark grayish brown to nearly black, often with clusters of large, many-branched thorns
- Twigs with branched thorns
- Fruit a large, curved, twisted pod

# HORSECHESTNUT   Marronnier d'Inde

Common horsechestnut
*Aesculus hippocastanum* L.
Hippocastanaceae: Horsechestnut Family

**Size and Form.** Horsechestnut is a medium-sized tree, 10 to 25 m high and 30 to 60 cm in diameter. Branches initially ascend from the trunk, bend downward as they lengthen, and terminate in coarse, upright twigs, forming a large, rounded or conical crown.

**Leaves.** Opposite, palmately compound with five to nine (normally seven to nine) obovate leaflets, 12 to 18 cm long, 3 to 6 cm wide, irregularly and bluntly toothed, thick, rough, dark

green above, pale beneath; sometimes with brown edges as the leaves dry on the tree. Leaflets stalkless, rachis long, grooved, and swollen at the base. Autumn color: yellow-orange.

**Bark.** Dark gray-brown, with irregular plates and shallow fissures, inner bark orange-brown.

**Twigs.** Very stout, smooth, light or reddish brown, with large white pores, leaf scar large, somewhat resembling a horseshoe with vein scars as nail holes.

**Buds.** Terminal bud large, 2 to 4 cm long, cone-shaped, sharp pointed, dark brown or purple-brown, sticky with a glistening gum; inner scales yellow, becoming 4 to 5 cm long in spring, clinging to the twig until the leaves are half grown.

**Flowers.** June, after the leaves; large white or cream-colored, in showy upright, branched terminal clusters 20 to 30 cm long and 10 to 20 cm wide, lateral stems jointed, with four to six flowers; five white petals spotted with yellow and red.

**Fruit.** A leathery spherical capsule about 5 cm in diameter, with short, flexible prickles, containing one to three large smooth chestnut-brown seeds, each with a large, pale circular area. Seed crops in most years. Not edible.

**Distribution.** A native of the Balkans, southeastern Europe, and the Himalayan areas of Asia; introduced into England in the early 1600s, widely planted in European parks and gardens; once widely planted in North America for its showy blooms and tolerance of urban conditions.

**Habitat.** Grows on a wide variety of sites, thrives in protected sites in colder parts of New England. Naturalized along roadsides and waste places in southern New England.

**Notes:** The species name *hippocastanum* means "horsechestnut," from the Greek hippos (horse) and kastanon (chestnut). The wood is light, soft, and weak, easily worked, once used in Europe for food containers, kitchen utensils, and carving, but little used today. Seeds of horsechestnut were sent from Constantinople to Vienna, reaching England about 1625 and the American colonies about 1750.

> ### In the Field
> - Leaves palmately compound with seven to nine large, thick, dark-green leaflets
> - Large, showy clusters of white flowers in late spring
> - Very stout twigs
> - Terminal buds in winter large, sticky, purple-brown
> - Fruit a leathery capsule with flexible prickles containing one to three large chestnut-brown seeds with a light brown spot when mature

# *Glossary*

**Acorn:** The nut of the oak, usually partly enclosed by a hard, woody cap.

**Anther:** The pollen-bearing part of a flower.

**Appressed:** Lying flat against.

**Axil:** The angle between a leaf and stem.

**Berry:** A fleshy fruit that contains one or more small seeds.

**Bipinnate:** Doubly pinnately compound (see **Pinnately compound**).

**Bract:** A modified leaf at the base of a flower, fruit, or leaf.

**Branchlet:** The smallest division of a branch representing last season's growth.

**Cane:** A slender, woody stem, for example, of a raspberry plant, usually short-lived.

**Capsule:** A dry fruit containing one or more seeds, which usually splits at maturity, releasing the seeds.

**Catkin:** A spike of male or female flowers, often caterpillar-like and drooping.

**Clone:** A group of plants arising asexually from one plant and genetically identical to the original plant,

**Collateral:** Side by side, referring to buds.

**Compound leaf:** A leaf that is divided into separate leaflets.

**Cone:** Usually a woody structure with overlapping scales containing seeds of gymnosperms.

**Crenate:** A leaf margin with rounded to blunt teeth.

**Deciduous:** Not persistent, dropping off at the end of the growing season.

**Dioecious:** Having male and female flowers (unisexual) on different plants.

**Divergent:** Extending outward from each other or from a point.

**Drupe:** A simple, one-seeded fleshy fruit with a bony inner wall.

**Entire:** Without teeth or lobes, as the margin of a leaf.

**Epicormic branch:** Usually a small branch arising from a dormant bud in the main stem or branch of a tree.

**Gymnosperms:** Bearing naked seeds; specifically referring here to the plant order *Coniferales*.

**Inflorescence:** A flower cluster.

**Lanceolate:** Shaped like a lance, longer than broad, tapering at the tip.

**Lenticel:** A circular or linear corky mark in the bark of woody plants originating as a breathing pore.

**Mesic:** Site or habitat water condition, intermediate between wet and dry.

**Monoecious:** Having male and female flowers (unisexual) on the same plant.

**Naturalized:** Spreading without cultivation to areas outside its native range.

**Nut:** A hard, closed, usually one-seeded fruit.

**Oblong:** Longer than broad with margins nearly parallel.

**Obovate:** Inverted ovate.

**Ovate:** Egg-shaped, broader at the base.

**Palmately compound:** A leaf with three or more leaflets radiating from a common point, like a palm tree.

**Pedicel:** The stalk of a single flower.

**Perennial plant:** One that lives year after year.

**Perfect flower:** One that contains both male and female parts.

**Petiole:** The stalk or stem of a leaf.

**Pinnately compound:** A leaf that has leaflets arranged along one central stalk or rachis.

**Pith:** Soft, central portion of a twig or stem.

**Polygamous:** Bearing perfect or unisexual flowers on the same or separate plants.

**Polygamo-dioecious:** Bearing perfect and either male or female flowers (unisexual) on separate plants.

**Polygamo-monoecious:** Bearing perfect and unisexual flowers on the same plant.

**Pome:** A fleshy fruit, such as an apple, with a central core containing seeds.

**Pubescent:** Covered with short, soft, downy hairs.

**Rachis:** The central stem of a compound leaf, spike, or flower cluster.

**Recurved:** Curved downward or backward.

**Rhizome:** An underground stem.

**Samara:** A nonsplitting, winged fruit.

**Serrate:** Having teeth pointing forward, as along a leaf margin.

**Sessile:** Without a stalk, attached directly to twig or stem.

**Simple leaf:** A single leaf, not divided into leaflets.

**Sinus:** The indentation between two lobes of a leaf.

**Spike:** An unbranched, elongated cluster of sessile flowers.

**Stipule:** A small appendage that occurs at the base of a leaf petiole, usually in pairs.

**Stolon:** A basal branch or runner, rooting at the nodes.

**Striate:** With fine grooves or lines.

**Taproot:** Primary descending root.

## Sources of Information

We used several standard sources for tree taxonomy, botanical features, ecology, distribution, and illustrations. Taxonomy follows that in D. Magee and H. Ahles, *Flora of the Northeast* (1999, University of Massachusetts Press, Amherst). Botanical features are from B. V. Barnes and W. H. Wagner, Jr., *Michigan Trees: A Guide to the Trees of Michigan and the Great Lakes Region* (2002, University of Michigan, Ann Arbor); G. P. DeWolf, Jr., *Native and Naturalized Trees of Massachusetts* (1996, University of Massachusetts Extension Service, Amherst); J. L. Farrar, *Trees of the Northern United States and Canada* (1995, Iowa State Press, Ames); and W. M. Harlow and E. S. Harrar, *Textbook of Dendrology*, fifth edition (1968, McGraw-Hill Book Company, New York). Tree distribution and ecology follows that in E. L. Little, Jr., *Atlas of American Trees*, vol. 1, *Conifers and Important Hardwoods* (1971, U.S. Department of Agriculture Misc. Pub. No. 1146, Washington, D.C.); R. M. Burns and B. H. Hankala, *Silvics of North American Trees*, vol. 1, *Conifers*, and vol. 2, *Hardwoods* (1990, U.S. Department of Agriculture Handbook 654, Washington, D.C.); and D. J. Leopold, *Trees of New York State: Native and Naturalized* (2003, Syracuse University Press, Syracuse), and *Forest Trees of Maine*, twelfth edition (1995, Maine Forest Service, Augusta). Useful information for "Notes" was obtained from V. Barlow in *Northern Woodlands:* Pin Cherry, *Prunus pennsylvanica* (Autumn 1999): 33; Red Pine, *Pinus resinosa* (Winter 1999): 53; Black Spruce, *Picea mariana* (Winter 2001): 35; Black Ash, *Fraxinus nigra* (Summer 2003): 28; Eastern Redcedar, *Juniperus virginiana* (Winter 2004): 37. The range maps for this book are derived from those in E .L. Little Jr., *Atlas of American Trees;* J. L. Farrar's *Trees of the Northern United States and Canada;* and D. Magee and H. Ahles, *Flora of the Northeast.* Illustrations of most species are from the N. L. Britton and A. Brown, *Illustrated Flora of the Northern States and Canada, and the British Possessions,* second edition, vols. I, II, and III (1913, New York: Charles Scribner's Sons) as provided in the USDA-NRCS

PLANTS Database, version 3.5 *http://plants.usda.gov*. Those of apple, black cherry, European mountain-ash, mockernut hickory, northern white-cedar, and weeping willow are reprinted with permission from H. P. Brown, *Trees of New York State: Native and Naturalized,* Tech. Pub. No. 15 (1921, the New York State College of Forestry at Syracuse University, Syracuse). Original illustrations of Norway spruce, Austrian pine, Norway maple, Scots pine, blue spruce, downy serviceberry, and showy mountain-ash are by Nancy Haver.

# Index

# Index

All species are listed by both their Latin and preferred English names, as well as by their French names, with the most general term first (e.g., *Acer* not *negundo;* oak, not red). Under the English names, the preferred common name is given in plain text with other common names in parentheses.